The THREE QUESTIONS

The THREE QUESTIONS

*How to Discover and Master
the Power Within You*

Don Miguel Ruiz and Barbara Emrys

HarperOne
An Imprint of HarperCollins*Publishers*

HarperOne

HarperCollins books may be purchased for educational, business, or
sales promotional use. For information, please email the Special Markets
Department at SPsales@harpercollins.com.

FIRST HARPERCOLLINS PAPERBACK EDITION PUBLISHED IN 2019

Designed by Yvonne Chan
Design treatments inspired by original artwork by Nicholas Wilton/Illustration Source

Library of Congress Cataloging-in-Publication Data is available upon
request.

ISBN 978-0-06-239108-7

23 24 25 26 27 LBC 12 11 10 9 8

This book is dedicated to those who have chosen to be the heroes of their own story. It is dedicated to all peaceful rebels who wish to change their world.

This book is dedicated to those who love themselves without condition and who let that pure love shine for the world. It is dedicated to those who lead with compassion, who dare to act kindly, and who will not be governed by irrational fear.

This book is dedicated to all women and men who act with courage and speak for those who cannot speak for themselves. It is written in honor of those who use their words to deliver messages of love and respect.

With heartfelt thanks to our readers,
DON MIGUEL RUIZ AND BARBARA EMRYS

CONTENTS

Introduction

Question 1: Ask Yourself, "Who Am I?"

Question 2: Ask Yourself, "What Is Real?"

CONTENTS

INTRODUCTION

I

The Three Pearls of Wisdom

ONE RAINY DAY, long ago, an old man was driving his wagon down a country road. The road was filled with potholes, so the drive was difficult, and the rain only made it worse.

As the wagon plunged into a particularly deep hole, a rear wheel broke off. Calming his horse, the old man jumped down onto the muddy road and began to struggle with the wagon wheel. He soon realized that the hole was too deep and the wheel was too heavy for him to lift. As he stood there, wet and cold, he heard footsteps running toward him.

A farm boy was on his way home to supper when he saw the old man's broken wagon, with water flowing around it like a river. The boy was big, strong, and eager to help. Finding a fallen fence post, he stepped knee-deep into the muddy hole and propped up the wagon. Then he began fixing the wheel.

While he worked, the boy spoke to the old man about his wishes for the future. He understood very little about the world, but he wanted to learn. He wanted to discover who he was and to find answers to life's biggest mysteries. He was going to be a man soon and wanted to know more about love. He said he often daydreamed about the wonderful things yet to come.

"Most days," the boy laughed, "I'm not sure if I'm dreaming or if I'm awake!" The boy talked on, and the old man listened in silence.

Within an hour, the job was done. The wheel was set securely in its place, and the wagon was back on the road. The old man, filled with gratitude, searched through his pockets for a few coins. Finding nothing to offer the boy for his work, he asked him if he would accept three pearls of wisdom instead, assuring him that the pearls would provide more riches than any coins. As the sun pierced through rushing storm clouds, the boy smiled. He knew he could not refuse the man's gratitude, however it was offered. And, after all, he had much to learn.

"Yes," answered the boy politely. "I am truly honored that you would share your wisdom with me, sir."

So the old man leaned toward him and began to speak.

"To find your way in this world you need only answer three questions," the old man explained. "First, you must ask yourself: 'Who am I?' You will know who you are when you see who you are not.

"Second, you must ask yourself: 'What is real?' You will know what is real when you accept what is not real.

"Third," the man finished, "you must ask yourself: 'What is love?' You will know love when you realize what love is not."

The old man straightened himself, brushing flecks of mud off his coat. The boy removed his hat respectfully and expressed his thanks. He watched the old man climb onto his wagon and whistle to his horse. The wagon lurched, shuddered, and then began to rattle down the road.

As the boy turned toward home, where supper was waiting, he glanced back to see the back of the wagon disappear among the evening shadows.

2

Opening the Door

SIMPLE STORIES INVITE us to reflect on our own lives. One way or another, they represent everyone's story. If a story is good, it has the power to inspire questions and encourage us to look for answers. If a story is very good, it can get under our skin and dare us to see the truth. It can open new doors of perception. These stories leave us a choice: to be challenged by the truth or to close the door and continue walking a familiar path.

This book is for those who are willing to see the truth of themselves. It is for those willing to ask what is real and to go through unfamiliar doors. *Life* is eager to begin a new conversation with you. If you're willing to listen and to change, your world can be transformed.

We humans are what we are today because of the way our nervous system has responded to light over millions of years. Our brains have become intricate, our capabilities diverse, and our societies complex. We've certainly made our mark on this planet. And yet, if we were asked what we had to show for humanity's years of evolution, what would we say?

Would we say that we're free of worry and conflict? Would we say we finally understand how to be the best humans we can be? It would be wonderful to say that our beliefs no longer drive us to do terrible things. It would be great to say that our minds no longer wage their internal wars. It would be nice to say that humans have become far too wise to turn against each other. It would be nice to say that about our species, but we cannot—not yet, at least.

In an ideal world, humans get along with each other for their own benefit and for the benefit of humanity. In an ideal community, people cooperate in order to prosper, and they appreciate their good fortune. They value life and care for the land that nurtures them. Ideally, they respect themselves and everyone else.

In an ideal family, children are made to feel safe and appreciated. Parents are inspired teachers and vigilant protectors. The elderly continue to be productive. Groups of people form societies, of course, but no society tries to undermine any other. Together, they build greater communities, and together they ensure the well-being of every citizen.

In this world of our imagination, governments may still exist. An ideal government presides over a country with respect. Its leaders are wise and far-seeing. The best possible congress is one that legislates with conscience and compassion. Its laws are clear and just—and the rules apply to everyone.

In this ideal world, people are also able to govern themselves justly. What does it mean to govern ourselves? It means we are in charge of our own thoughts and responsible for our own actions. We refuse to walk blindly through life. We see exactly what is and not merely what we prefer to see. We don't permit the past to take command of the present. We view our personal reality the way a great artist would—with an eye for beauty and balance.

In an ideal world, we don't punish ourselves repeatedly for one mistake. We don't indulge in self-pity. We don't manipulate emotions. We don't gossip or seek out drama.

In an ideal world, we have no desire to judge or to blame. We are not defeated by guilt and shame, nor do we inflict shame on anyone else. In other words, we govern ourselves in the same way we want to be governed: with respect.

There is much more we could say about that ideal world, but it's important to consider why this world doesn't actually exist for most of us. Helping the world move toward its ideal expression is too great a task for a small book, but we can take the first steps on our own. Everything we build together as human beings begins with a little imagination. We may believe we are tragic victims of circumstance, but with imagination we can take another perspective and see how unkindly we treat ourselves. With all its thoughts and judgments, the mind may seem like our worst adversary, but by imagining the mind differently, we can make it our ally. By modifying the way our minds work we can begin to change our world.

We all have fears we won't admit to ourselves, and we're not always sure how to overcome them. We need love, but we're not convinced we deserve it. We want to love ourselves, but we don't know how. To one degree or another, there is chaos and confusion in each of us. Ideas take hold, and opinions intimidate. We get caught up in our own drama and take it all so seriously. We play roles that don't reflect the truth of what we are.

Why do we do this to ourselves? The answer is that we were shown how, and we became masters at it.

Everyone is born an authentic being, but it is hard to remain authentic in a world where beliefs have already been assigned to us. As infants and children, we are told who we are, how we should behave, and how to respond to what we perceive. This is how families and cultures function most effectively and how children survive within their cultures. But that doesn't mean these lessons are rooted in reality. You could say that our early training teaches us to deceive ourselves. We learn to lie.

Life is truth, and only *life* exists. By using words to describe the truth, we automatically distort it. So a lie is simply a distortion of the truth. There may be no malice intended, but we still use lies against ourselves and against each other.

We all know how little kids say the funniest things—funny, because they speak the truth as they perceive it, without judgment. Honest insights, plainly spoken, sound pretty shocking to adult ears. Why? In many cultures, stating an obvious truth is considered impolite. Honesty and authenticity are sometimes thought to be childlike qualities. At times, they might even be considered crazy. Most of us have learned to lie about what we see and how we feel. By the time we've reached adulthood, we've even learned to believe our lies.

Growing up, we develop strong minds, but minds can become corrupted. We form strong opinions, but our opinions don't represent the truth. Emotional responses become corrupted when they are ruled by opinions and beliefs. We were created by a loving force, but we even learn to corrupt love.

Corruption sounds like a willful crime, but people don't come into the world with corrupt intentions. We were born hungry for the truth and eager to love. Corruption happens when we put our faith in thoughts and ideas instead of what we perceive. We believe most of what we're told and, in the process, we lose our connection with *life*—with truth. We create rules and structures that conform to what we've been taught to believe.

Love is one example of how our natural impulses can be poisoned by ideas. Too many of us were taught that love is conditional, that it comes with specific rules of engagement. To put it simply, love is corrupted by *if*.

We may not always hear *if* spoken out loud, but we sense it often enough, even between people who are devoted to each other.

- I will love you *if* you do what I want.
- I'll love you *if* you stand by me, no matter what.
- I'll love you *if* you do this or believe that.
- *If* you embarrass me, disagree with me, or leave me . . . I will stop loving you.

Amazingly, we say things like this to the people we care about most, just as we say them to ourselves. Yes, we set conditions on loving ourselves—conditions that are often too strict to meet. Real love comes with no conditions. And yet that's not how most of us were taught to offer love and to receive it.

When we think of love as conditional, it becomes something else, something corrupt. Of course, this kind of corruption can be repaired, because it begins in the virtual world of the mind. Virtual reality is a reflection, an interpretation of what is real.

The mind gives us an impression of everything we can touch and see, but it's an impression. Ideas aren't made of matter. Beliefs aren't part of our genetic makeup. The mind isn't actually real, and the fanciful world it creates doesn't actually exist.

So what is the mind, and what does it do?

The mind is a function of the brain that turns perception into language. The ways we describe reality are unique to each of us. You have your way; I have mine. The difference depends on how our brains work, of course. It also depends on how we've been taught to perceive the world.

When we see an idyllic scene—such as a mountain range, green meadows, and open expanses of wilderness—some of us think of paradise. We react with excitement and pleasure. Others, seeing the same scenery, imagine extreme hardship and loneliness and react in fear. Where some see tranquility, others see disturbance. If we were taught to be afraid, we will likely continue to be afraid. If we believe that unfamiliar things are dangerous, we will avoid new experiences.

We were taught to interpret what we see. We were told what to believe and believed what we were told. We've been guided by private and public opinion since we were born. Reality is made of impressions and experiences to which we give personal meaning and value. It changes constantly, of course, since events keep changing. Our personal perception of reality is affected by our opinions and our fears.

Many beliefs encourage fear. Many beliefs are influenced by fear. Fear has had a big effect on the way we learned to view the world. Physical fear is natural and essential to our survival, but it's important to remember that irrational fear is not. It is irrational to be afraid of what doesn't exist. In fact, it can cause actual harm. And yet we've learned to let irrational fear shape our reality. We've learned to react emotionally in ways that other people do and to fear what we only imagine.

These reactions took time and practice to perfect. We followed the rules of our families and cultures. Our parents and teachers showed us how to behave in a world of humans, and we took those lessons with us into adulthood. Now we tell ourselves how to behave in much the same way. We follow the rules of society, but we've applied most of society's rules to our own lives. We rule ourselves through self-made laws, personal judgments, and mental intimidation.

As children, we observed how our own family and our local community were governed. We followed the protocols of school, church, and the front office. To go against the rules usually resulted in a loss of respect among our peers. Sometimes the losses were far greater. We obeyed the rules of our city and state governments and the laws of our nation's government. Breaking those rules meant paying bigger penalties. All of this influenced the way our minds work, and so you could say the way we run ourselves mirrors the way things run in the world.

It's no surprise that we all have a little government operating in our heads. The mind is the government that sets the rules, and the physical body follows those rules. We're willing to pay real penalties for breaking the rules we put in place—and, very often, we make someone else pay as well. Like most governments, the mind tries to impose its laws on other bodies.

When we are aware of the way the mind functions, we can alter the way we rule ourselves. When we see how our own little government works, we can change it. We can amend our own laws. Whatever we're able to imagine for our own sake we can create. We can become better caretakers to our bodies and allow ourselves more freedom of expression. We can end the strict penalties we've inflicted on ourselves— penalties that make it impossible to experience the love we deserve.

We all want to be the best humans we can be. We want to contribute to our own personal evolution. We want to know what we've been doing wrong and what we could do better. We want our secret questions to be answered and to see how the answers can be applied to our own lives. We'd like to discover what is true.

We can all use a few pearls of wisdom. Wisdom improves our relationship with *life*, with truth. It allows us to rise above our fears and our common beliefs. It gives us the will to walk through one new door, and then the next.

The journey begins with three essential questions:

- Who am I?
- What is real?
- What is love?

ASK YOURSELF, "WHO AM I?"

3

The First Pearl

*Who am I? You will know who you are
when you see who you are not.*

WE THINK WE know all there is to know about
ourselves. You may believe you're the reliable one,
the optimistic one, or the melancholy one. You've
probably decided you're either an introvert or the life
of the party. Sometimes we experience a disturbance
of some kind in our lives, a trauma or a loss. See-

ing ourselves in action during a crisis, we're sometimes shocked. It could be that we never imagined we could be so strong. Or maybe we're weaker than we expected or more fearful. There comes a time in most of our lives when we're ready to admit we are not who we thought we were.

In such cases, it could be that the values we defend aren't reflected in our actions. We're in conflict with people around us. Our minds are in conflict with our hearts. We blame or we lash out. We shout at our kids. We insult a friend. "Where did that come from?" we ask ourselves. Confused and discouraged, we begin to wonder what makes us do the things we do. We wanted the truth but seemed to have missed something in our search.

Asking yourself, "Who am I?" means taking the first step back to authenticity, or truth. Our instinct is to cling to the picture we have of ourselves, which makes any new discoveries impossible. Questioning who we are gives us a chance to bring down a few walls—a few stubborn beliefs—and reconnect with *life*.

Most of the stories about who you are come from things your parents told you—what you like, what you dislike, or what you're good at. You heard more opinions from brothers, sisters, and childhood friends. As you grew up, you got descriptions of yourself from everyone you met. "You're the smart one," they might have said. "You're the rebel," or "My, you're just like your father." People still like to imagine you in their own way. "You're so stubborn," "You don't know how to love," "You never take risks."

By now, you've formed a solid opinion of yourself, but consider what that opinion is based on. Since you were born, you've heard different people describe you many different ways. They each see what they want to see. And you've supplemented other people's stories with stories of your own. When you meet someone, you talk about your life—past events and hopes for the future. You tell the same stories, more or less the same way, featuring yourself as the main character. How did that character come to define you? Let's first look at how we tell our story, and then we can see how the main character describes itself and drives all our actions.

We are storytelling creatures. Telling a story is a good way to connect to other people. Most of us don't think of ourselves as weavers of myths, but we never stop telling the story of our lives. We recount the events of each day as they unfold, for anyone who will listen. We tell stories to ourselves, as if to explain what we've already experienced. We talk nostalgically about yesterday and speculate about tomorrow. Some stories we tell often, inventing dramatic interpretations and new plot twists. And why not? Telling stories is what humans do.

You probably don't put faith in fairy tales anymore, but you believe the story of your life. Most of us put a lot of faith in our version of reality. We talk about the events of our lives reverently, describing them in careful detail. We put on a performance for an audience of one, or many. If we stopped to listen to ourselves, we'd also realize how masterfully we play with emotions. If we took the time to write down the story of our lives, highlighting its most important moments, we'd see how easy it is to fall into our own emotional traps. However, if we wrote it all down a second time and a third, those moments would eventually lose their power to move us. We would begin to see just how much we are shaping our story to emphasize the drama.

Even the best stories lose their emotional impact after the first telling. When we're finally able to disarm the emotional triggers in our own story, we can recall any event without the usual self-pity or self-importance. We can talk about today's problems and yesterday's mishaps without the need for sympathy. If we ever read our story out loud, we'd begin to see it all as a work of fiction, a work of art. And we'd realize that even our best stories don't tell the truth about us. So if that's the case, then *who are we?*

As the old man in our little parable suggested, we'd be wise to first take a look at what we are not.

4

The Voice of *Me*

EVER SINCE YOU can remember, you've given the main character of your story power to determine your reality. It has the authority to talk, think, and make decisions that affect your body and your world. It tells you what to believe and how to invest your beliefs with emotional energy. You call the main character in your ongoing story *me*.

Let's take a minute to understand what the word *me* means in this context. *Me* is the person you accept as your real self. You talk about yourself all the time, right? You say *me, mine,* and *myself* countless times in the course of an ordinary conversation. Through *me,* you say things like, "Hey, this is important to me!" or, "Are you listening to me?" or, "What are they saying about me?" *Me* is everything you believe you are. *Me* is everything related to the character you forged out of core beliefs and countless experiences.

The word *me,* or its counterpart in any language, is a simple pronoun—and like every word in the language we speak, it has no meaning until we agree upon a meaning. The difference is that *me* comes with a lot of baggage: past memories, judgments, and automatic assumptions. We put a lot of faith in our identity and expect it to matter to other people. Who we think we are develops into a mythology. We share the myth of *me* with old friends and new acquaintances. We tell riveting stories about ourselves. We send photos to back up our stories. We celebrate *me* in so many ways.

Me always refers to the person speaking, but we don't give much consideration to who that might be. We say, "Look at me!" indicating that we want attention given to this human being—but also to this thought process, these frustrations, these expectations. We feel sympathy for ourselves, but to the one listening, "Look at me!" could evoke other emotions. Our idea of who we are isn't everyone's idea of who we are. It may not be anyone's idea.

Me doesn't refer to the body we occupy. *Me* doesn't describe the energy that moves through us. *Me* isn't a primal thing, because we didn't invent a "self" until we learned a language. *Me* didn't exist until we began to see the world through symbols and their meanings. In short, *me* doesn't refer to anything real. It refers to an image, an idea we have of ourselves that we've attempted to put into words. Of course, the words we use to describe ourselves change all the time, because we see things differently with every changing situation. Who we think we are has evolved a lot since early childhood, when we first began to talk and think. Who we imagine ourselves to be still changes—with time, with shifting moods, and with the feedback we get from people we care about.

Our impressions change, but we each subscribe

to a general myth, or false belief, about ourselves. *Me* is a personal mythology, a collection of stories that we repeat to ourselves and accept as truth. Like children with their superheroes, we are believers in *me*. Wrapped in our mythology, we feel confident to take on the world.

Me is not what you actually are. You are *life*, or the energy that made you a physical being. *Life* runs through your body and makes it able to move, to love, to feel. *Life's* energy created your miraculous brain. It made a thinking mind possible and gave voice to its main character. *Life* is everything seen and unseen. Only *life* exists.

There is only *life*—and infinite points of view. Everything created by *life* has a point of view, and your body is one. Your mind is one. The human body develops according to its biological programming, but the mind evolves consciously, through attention and deliberate action. The mind is what we think we are, until we decide otherwise. The voice that speaks for the mind is us, until we recognize that it's not the truth of us at all.

Of all the things we can accomplish as humans, this kind of self-awareness brings the most rewards. It can guide the evolution of the main character. *Me* responds to your name and knows your history. *Me* is aware of your physical environment, and *me* can also become aware of itself.

Personal growth does get complicated when we try to distance ourselves from the character we created. Through *me*, we describe ourselves and the world. If we claim to be the victim of the voice in our head, we'll be the victim in all situations. If we deny the power we have to change the voice of *me*, how can new doors of awareness ever open? How can we live fearlessly within the dream of humanity, where there are more than seven billion *me*'s—all with opinions of their own and all demanding to be heard?

Reality is everyone's personal creation, so the same is true of your reality. The judgments in your head are the result of your beliefs and past experiences. If you feel oppressed by your own thoughts, then it's time to take charge of them. Does *me* have to be a big judge or a constant victim? No. Most of us want a closer relationship with the truth, and we all want some peace of mind. We want to be healthy, but so often our judgments make us sick. We want to be spiritually aware, but our beliefs keep us spellbound.

If we take the time to listen to what we think and say, we have a chance to be more honest with ourselves. Behavior follows belief, and any belief can be modified. If we challenge our own opinions, we can begin to find our way back to authenticity. Do we always have to be right? Do we really need to have the last word? If our actions do not represent the kind of people we want to be, we can take new paths of action. We can change.

It makes sense that the more we invest in our own self-image, the more difficult it is to change. So we shouldn't use the main character of our story as an excuse to feel victimized or to deceive ourselves. The truth can speak through the mind, just as it moves through nerves and flesh. The mind can choose to serve truth and not the stories. Life's energy uses the tools available to create a body, a thought, or a dream. A healthy body is a wonderful conduit for energy, and an aware mind is the secret to making our reality work for us.

Your body is real, but *me* is fictional. And yet *me* is running the show. How many times have you defended your actions and not understood why? At times, we all regret doing things we consider inexcusable or saying things we don't really mean. We like to say, "I'm only human," but it's not our humanness that's causing the problem. So it's natural to wonder who really is in charge. "Who am I?" we wonder, not really expecting an answer. No one stops to ask who they're *not*, and that's where we have to begin.

Be aware of yourself as energy, and everything changes. Here is how that works. You are no longer the victim of your beliefs; you are the creator. You are the artist. You are also the painting—the canvas that is your reality. Imagine picking up a brush and painting a figure that looks like you. Imagine doing that continually for the rest of your life. Unlike most figures in a painting, however, this one has a brain. It has a brain with a mind that gives meaning to what it perceives. It functions beautifully, but it's not aware that there is an artist. There are many other figures in this painting, but they're also not aware of the artist. This makes it inevitable that they rely on each other for knowledge. They react and interact with each other. They learn from each other.

Every day the scenario changes. Instant by instant, there are subtle changes happening to the painter's main point of focus. The figure itself is coming alive at your touch. You not only have colors and brushes to work with, but you can make choices through this character. You can work as *life* works, providing constant opportunity for growth, so that the main figure adapts well to an ever-changing landscape. You can skillfully guide *me* into awareness.

Some people dare to look inward. They take the time to listen to their own thoughts and reflect on their own actions. They ask questions of themselves. "Am I really this kind of person?"

"Are these feelings genuine?" "If I'd known I had a choice, would I have done it the same way?" They catch themselves in midreaction and change the response. They find emotional balance. That's what it means to be present. That's how we become healthier in mind and spirit. By observing, we can all learn. By modifying the voice in our heads, we have a chance to grow wise.

Some people stop believing their thoughts altogether. This is important, because once the voice in our head loses authority, it turns silent. We can observe events and respond genuinely. We're used to reacting in expected ways. We're used to seeing things as we've been taught to see them—and as we've preferred to see them. Once we stop lying to ourselves, all that is left is truth. All that is left is authenticity, something we lost in our storytelling.

Throughout human history, people have been wondering, questioning, seeking. Some of those people have changed the world—not just their world, but the entire dream of humanity. They begin by doubting what they know. They ask one question, then another. They consult wiser men and women, perhaps. Soon, they start listening to the main character of their own story. It has a voice that speaks clearly, and only to them. What is it saying, and how much of its message is true? Can any of it be believed? For that matter, what is the truth, what is real?

We have a few amazing tools to work with when it comes to solving the mystery of who we are. The first tool is the *power of attention*. Our attention is what makes it possible to take notice and to learn. The sound of our name captures our attention, a response we learned in infancy. Attention brings every other faculty into play—we look, we listen, we respond. We receive information, and we process it. And, by catching another person's attention, we learn to transmit information to someone else and out to the world.

Over time, however, we've mastered the art of sleepwalking through life. We don't think we need to pay attention, because we're sure we know what's going on around us. Our responses to everything have become predictable. Our thinking is automatic, and we automatically assume we know what other people are thinking. It's safe to say that our attention has been weakened by neglect. What if we rediscovered its amazing power? We'd have minds that are agile and flexible when events change—and change is inevitable.

There's no need ever to be crushed by failed expectations. If we used our senses to gather real information, we wouldn't be so mystified by life. If we really listened—not only to what people are saying, but also to what we say to ourselves in quiet moments—we would empathize with others so much more and show compassion toward ourselves. Instead, we make assumptions and encourage misunderstanding. Strengthening our attention may feel like a workout at first, but the rewards come quickly. The brain responds eagerly to new challenges. Look, listen, and observe without judgment. Notice how your emotional responses become more honest without a story. Attention can lead to total awareness in every precious moment of life.

The second tool is *memory*. Memory is stored in matter (our brains) the way music is stored on a compact disc. We're able to store all the memories of a lifetime in one brain, but that doesn't make those memories real. We store impressions of things, people, and events—but since every brain perceives in its own way, even siblings remember childhood events differently. Memory helps to create an impression of reality, but impressions aren't the same as truth. We rely too much on memory to tell us the truth. We let it turn our attention away from the present moment and draw us into the past. We frequently use memory against ourselves, but we have the power to use it differently. Instead, we can let memory enlighten us.

Just as memory played a key role in our early development, it can guide us in our adult transformation. In infancy we watched our parents; we listened, and we imitated. Everything we observed became part of our own pattern of behavior. We tried to walk, we fell down, and we tried again. We learned to avoid pain and move toward pleasure. And what about now, when we wish to change some unpleasant patterns? Why wouldn't we do everything we can to take care of our physical body and our emotional well-being? We know how it feels to lose our temper and feel regret. It feels awful. We know how shame and guilt make us feel, and yet we still invite them in. Memory can serve us in our efforts to wake up and resist automatic responses. Memory can steer us away from abusive habits, encouraging us to stand up and walk forward with self-respect.

The third and best tool is *imagination*. Imagination is its own kind of superpower. We picture something in our minds, and then we make it real. In fact, just by imagining something wonderful, the body feels comforted and energized. We can also imagine painful events and horrible consequences. By imagining the worst, we produce fear in the physical body and spread fear to other bodies. We imagine the future and tune out the present. Imagination is power, for sure; but like all power, it can be corrupted.

Right now, we can practice using imagination in a valuable way. We can turn our attention to the exciting task of making ourselves more aware. We can use memory the way it was intended to be used—to keep us from repeating past mistakes. We can imagine things we've never tried to imagine. We can doubt what we know and let go of familiar stories. The mind wields enormous influence. It has developed habits over time, but we can change those habits. By using the tools available to us, we can calm the inner chaos and find peace in our virtual world.

You're not who you think you are. In obvious ways, you're not the kid you were at four years old, struggling with unspoken fears. You're not the awkward teen, the rookie at work, or the young entrepreneur. You're not someone's significant other or your mom's favorite child. You're not the main character of your story or anyone else's, regardless of how long you've played those roles. And you're not actually the one you call *me*, who tries to speak for your physical body. You're not your mind or the set of laws your mind tries so hard to enforce. It has created an entire governing force out of those laws, but that's not what you are either.

You're not really the little government in your head, but its laws nonetheless influence your actions and reactions. Sometimes that government seems tolerant; sometimes it's blind and unforgiving. Either way, *me* is operating as its commander in chief.

Now would be a good time to decide what kind of leader *me* should be. Now is a good time to take a look at your creation and to make inspired changes.

We were all born to learn, to grow, and to become aware human beings. It was our intention to be the best we could be. Somewhere along the way, we got distracted. Our intentions were derailed. We forgot what it felt like to be authentic. It may seem impossible to escape from our own system of punishments and rewards, but that's not true. We can bring down the whole structure if we want to.

It's interesting to see how each of us creates a personal reality. It's also interesting to see just how far we go to defend that reality. Rather than defend it, we can make it better. It takes a few basic insights to pull off a revolution. First, it's important to see how the system was put into place. It's helpful to see how we got here, wherever we are, and what we can do to change our world. We can explore ways to transform the one who's describing that world to us.

Awareness is the ability to see what is, and it's never too late to open our eyes.

5

One Mind, One Community

To UNDERSTAND THE governing mind a little better, let's first take another look at the ways in which
we've been governed throughout our lives. We were
each born into a vast community called humanity.
Over many thousands of years, humans have created
groups, or civilizations, all over the planet. We create groups in order to survive. We agree on certain
rules—written laws or ritual customs—so that order
can be maintained within those groups. We establish

governing bodies made up of respected men and women. We create cities and nations, all run by their own government. Every nation is made of smaller governing bodies, and it all starts with the family.

A family is its own little nation, traditionally composed of a man, a woman, and their children. A family cannot be defined any one way, of course—a family is formed when people of different genders and ages come together in order to provide for the welfare and safety of the group. The group may consist of two people, a dozen people, or many more. Together they create a home, which is an extension of themselves. Every family is regulated by its own government. Families establish rules of conduct, rules that help maintain harmony within the group: "Work hard," "Look after each other," "Respect your elders." They also devise punishments for breaking those rules. The head of a family makes key decisions, setting the rules and enforcing them.

One parent may yield authority to the other, or both parents may share power equally, forming government within the family. You and I were born to

different families and grew up in different house-
holds. The rules were probably different, along with
penalties for bad behavior, but we were both domesticated using a system of punishments and rewards.
From the time we were toddlers, we learned there
was a price to pay for rebellion. Whoever served as
the head the family imposed the rules, using the
power of authority.

Of course, those in charge had other ways of per-
suading us. They might have applied physical punishments or psychological abuses. Sometimes, all it
took was the subtle power of suggestion. Using our
own imaginations to control us, our parents often
told stories about naughty kids getting what they
deserved. "You'd better watch out," they cautioned
us, using Santa Claus, the bogeyman, or dead saints
to make their point. Parents tell stories to manage
their children. To discipline unruly children, they
intimidate. To keep them from danger, they use
whatever means they think is appropriate. Parents
themselves are ruled by the strict lessons of their
childhood. No one is above the law.

Groups of families create communities, the next level of government. A community, like a family, is dedicated to the welfare of the whole. Every community has a leader, just as every family does, and that leader makes the rules regarding acceptable modes of behavior. Everyone in the community agrees to follow the rules, knowing they will receive some kind of punishment if they don't.

When communities create alliances with other communities, cities are established. In a city, there are many more people who want to lead. The competition gets fierce, and governing becomes more arduous. Every city must choose a mayor and a legislature made up of dedicated citizens. Together, they decide on the rules of acceptable conduct and on various ways of enforcing those rules. Cities are ruled by their individual governments, and no one person—not even the mayor—is above the law.

When cities develop partnerships with other cities, a province or a state is formed. Every state has its own government, which has its own governor and system of laws. Choosing leaders gets more complicated as societies get larger. Citizens find it harder to be active participants in their own fate. Governors administer justice according to state laws and enforce those laws through whatever force is available to them. No one (at least in theory) is above the law.

States ultimately form a confederacy called a country or nation. Now the stakes are high for everyone. Different kinds of government leaders compete to rule the entire country. Once in office, they use the power of their authority and direct available forces to impose their rules. Enforcement doesn't always mean imprisonment or corporeal punishment. Governors may also use fear and imagination to manage their constituents. Like their parents once did, they might use threats, guilt, and shame. They may simply use little suggestions to influence people. By whatever means, they enforce the law. And they often find that they are not above the laws they've put in place.

A leader of one nation may desire to rule other nations as well. This is how civilizations evolve, as societies become more complex and leaders expand their authority. Nations form bigger nations and impose their laws on more communities and families. In some cases, nations lose power and get swallowed up. Maps are drawn and redrawn. Rules still continue to be made and enforced, with whatever means are available.

It's worthwhile to remember how outside governance has played a continuing role in our lives. It's worthwhile because our personal reality reflects the ways we use the same governing methods to discipline ourselves. We've been taught to respond to traffic lights, signals, and sirens—because by not responding we risk paying a penalty. We don't ignore tax deadlines or no-trespassing signs for the same reason. In any country, life goes more smoothly when we don't challenge local laws. Challenging our own mental directives is another matter. Thinking that harsh judgment is somehow virtuous, we impose rules and sanctions on ourselves, rarely stopping to wonder why. Would it hurt if we relaxed our control a little? What price would we pay for being kinder to ourselves?

We grew up under the influence of one governing institution after another. We all learned by observing, listening, and imitating—so it follows that
we've devised a way to police our own happiness.
We are afraid to lose control. We want to control
other people without considering their freedoms or
showing them basic respect. Too often, our system
of governing gets in the way of our basic desire to
communicate and to love.

It's not surprising that our principles—the ones
taught to us by our family and culture—often sup-
press us and put limits on our joy. Imitating them,
we write our own constitution and execute our own
punishments. We disparage ourselves, attack ourselves, and suffer the emotional pain. For reasons
most of us have forgotten, we insist on denying our
bodies basic pleasures. We often force ourselves to
do what we don't enjoy, and we (sometimes literally)
send ourselves to bed without supper. In the personal reality we've created, no one is above the law.
Not even us.

Imposing our will on other people only pushes

them away. Our laws aren't real. Our little government only illustrates who we are not. We're not lawmakers, doomed to enforce rules at the expense of our own happiness. Our minds and bodies are meant to be allies in the quest for a better relationship with *life*. By questioning our own rules, we can enjoy the freedom to act and react truthfully. We can start the journey back to authenticity.

6

The Mind as Government

ALLOWING THE MIND to operate like a government pulls us farther from what we really are. Devising laws and punishments is a job for outside institutions. It is what societies do, and even their success depends on a willingness to change what doesn't work. With all our private judgments and censures, we've each built virtual jails for ourselves—and that can't possibly make us happy.

Our personal reality doesn't have to be a prison. It

should be an artistic effort. When we think of it as a living work of art, we can modify the masterpiece as we go. We have the power to make better choices, keeping the welfare of the body in mind. By governing ourselves with respect, we can create harmony in every facet of our lives. Of course, it helps to remind ourselves what government was designed to do.

The kind of government most of us are familiar with has three main branches: a legislative, an executive, and a judicial branch. All three have the overriding purpose of serving the welfare of the country. A system of checks and balances makes sure one branch of government doesn't act in ways that undermine the others. Our mind can work the same way, by checking the integrity of its own actions. Every branch needs to be accountable and transparent. The mind needs to be aware of itself and practice effective oversight.

The legislative branch of any government is called *congress*. Congress makes laws and ratifies treaties, and so does the human mind. The mind creates strict laws—not just those handed down by family and society, but its own laws. These laws—whether consciously or unconsciously made—govern how we live. They're the self-reprimands and resolutions that guide our behavior. They also include our prejudices and phobias. You abide by the laws of your mind, and your mind expects others to abide by its laws as well. As you may have noticed, you get along better with people who respect your laws and accept your views.

Take a moment to consider how much importance you give to your rules and principles. It doesn't matter if they echo the principles of your parents or grandparents, because they're yours now. You may be able to state them clearly, and you may find fault with people who don't agree with those principles. You may even try to convince family members and friends to follow them. If they disagree, you might get angry. You might even pick a fight.

As it turns out, most relationship problems have to do with your government wanting to be right and deciding every other government is wrong. Defending your own constitution, you often declare war on other nations and their people. Most people declare a thousand little wars over a lifetime, fighting every criticism and rival opinion. You get the sense that you're not being respected, so you become disrespectful. All of this inhibits your natural inclination to love and be generous. Your *congress* has overruled your authenticity, which means your government has defeated its true purpose.

We lose our sense of fairness and empathy when our personal laws take on too much importance. It's nice to have a code of behavior to live by, but that code should not have a negative impact on our relationships. We may not even recognize certain ideas as principles, but the character called *me* still uses them to legislate and to prosecute. It uses them to scold other people and to quarrel with itself. Understanding our own actions and reactions makes a change in our internal government possible.

Think about the ideas that define you—ideas that tell the world who you are. You're an activist or a volunteer. You're a workaholic. You're a liberal or a conservative. You're loyal to a fault. You're God-fearing, patriotic, and the number-one fan of your home team. These may seem like admirable ways to describe yourself, but have they made your life easier? How much time do you spend explaining and defending your position? Do you criticize people who describe themselves differently? Do you "lay down the law" to your family and friends, expecting them to be as fanatical as you are? You may still want to start a war or just win a few battles. Either way, opinions aren't where your power lies. They're just opinions. A good argument is still just an argument.

Your beliefs and ideologies may feel as if they are the heart and soul of you, but they're not. Cherished ideas represent a way of thinking that makes us feel safe and possibly even superior. We invest them with a lot of emotional power, but they have no power of their own. Ideas and ideologies influence the way we conduct ourselves, which often feels right, but they can also harm our ability to interact and share time with others.

Think about your beliefs. Are they more important than the truth of you? Are they more precious than love?

To respect someone's right to an opinion is an act of love. It's a gift to others to let them share their views. It's not so difficult to listen without judgment. It's not that weird to say, "I don't know," and disarm the moment. Let others know they have a valid point. We don't always have to be right. We don't ever have to be *me*.

Most of the battles we fight are in our heads. We grapple with ideas and constantly struggle with notions of right and wrong. And then we take the fight outside, arguing about truth and lies, good and evil. Our way is brilliant; their way is stupid. Like most conflicts between nations, our wars with other people are public declarations of self-importance.

We have a tendency to defend the main character of our story, often as if we were defending human life. Consider that for a moment: we're defending the integrity of something that isn't real. Maybe we're afraid of losing face, and that reveals the whole problem. We will lose our masks, in other words. We will abandon pretense. Unable to support what we are not, we will stand naked and authentic in front of the world—which may be what we've needed all along.

If we refuse to quit old habits and pretenses, how can we experience the truth of us? We will continue to be at odds with the world. We will continue to see injustice everywhere and make our lives that much more difficult. The voice of *me* insists that we be right and that everyone else be wrong, but where do our ideas come from in the first place? If we dare to incorporate new ideas, what exactly is at stake? Who needs to be shielded from that disturbance? If we want peace of mind, we won't find it by arguing and insisting.

We find unexpected peace when we stop trying to defend the main character.

7

Justice and the Judge

MAKING LAWS IS up to congress, one branch of government. We can say that the mind acts as a legislative branch, but the mind invents ways to implement its laws as well. So let's turn to the second branch of self-government: the judicial.

The judicial branch decides how laws should be enforced and under what circumstances. Like outside governments, our mental government demands punishment for breaking the law. We have many different ways of exacting punishments on the people around us. Our punishments may be subtle or brutal, or we may turn our anger against ourselves. How many of us have tortured ourselves for eating too much, accomplishing too little, or for just not being good enough?

People run their judicial systems differently. You may be tough on yourself, but lenient with others. You might be clueless about your own crimes, but highly sensitive to the crimes of other people. You may be a loving person to others, but cruel to yourself—or the other way around. Most people are capable of cruelty if they're angry or insecure enough. Before you can make changes to your particular justice system, you need to acknowledge how it works.

We all need to consider our actions. We can ask ourselves, "Is this response fair? Am I being respectful in this situation? Would I want to be treated this way?"

Respect is a word that's impressed on us in childhood, but we were never given a chance to understand it fully. In spite of what many of us were told, no one has to *earn* respect. Everyone is different, but every human body is a copy of *life* itself. Every creature gives proof to the dance of energy and matter—that's reason enough to show respect. Respect makes it possible to see beyond someone's opinions and customs. It makes it possible to see the truth, and truth frees us from our deceptions.

There's no real justice when a government is operating blindly. When the mind is reacting automatically, we make errors in judgment. We pay a high price for our assumptions, causing unnecessary suffering. If we refuse to see things as they are, we can get disappointed. We blame, and we carry grudges. We show contempt for ourselves and others. How does any of this make us better human beings? How does this make us feel safer or more at peace with ourselves?

Respect is the solution to injustice. Heaven, by any interpretation, is ruled by respect. We create heaven on earth by respecting ourselves and every living thing. Respect makes our interactions with other people go more smoothly. At home, in our social lives, and in our business dealings, respect wins allies. We don't have to like people to show them respect. All human relationships thrive on mutual respect, whether or not we can agree on ideas.

We can't give what we don't have, so respect has to begin with us. Not all of us were taught self-respect in childhood. We may not have been encouraged to respect our bodies and the bodies of other humans. As adults, we can now assess how kind we are to ourselves. How fair are we? How severe is our justice system, particularly when it comes to our own behavior? Can we forgive ourselves? Do we even know how?

Just as forgiveness is essential to bring healing to a country, it is also essential to a healthy mind. Throughout human history, the practice of forgiveness has turned mortal enemies into compassionate allies. This happens in our own lives as well. Forgiveness puts old grievances to rest. We often resist the impulse to forgive, because we think it absolves bad people from a just punishment. Guilt or innocence is not the point. Forgiveness releases each of us from the need to hate.

Forgiveness takes the past off our shoulders, so we can go forward without its burden. For nations and individuals alike, the past is a corpse we shouldn't want to carry around with us. Memory should teach, not torture us. We want to be well again, happy and whole. By forgiving a trespass, we release ourselves from torment.

Consider the way you use past memories to hurt yourself, time and again. There's no justice in any of it. You feel the pain over and over, and no one is affected but you. Remembering makes you miserable, and life becomes miserable for those close to you. You overlook the present moment until it too becomes the past. The future becomes clouded by hatred. All the real moments are lost to the moments that never existed. So, of course, you feel you've missed something.

We were all domesticated through a system of rewards and punishments. The rewards might have been positive attention for our behavior—words of praise or gestures of affection. We might have been treated to ice cream for a job well done or allowed to spend a day playing outside with a friend. "Punishment" could mean a lack of response from our parents or harsh words. A punishment might have meant getting spanked or being subjected to worse physical abuses. But it also felt like punishment to us when we were blamed for something or made to feel guilty and ashamed.

As adults, we've learned to reward ourselves for our good deeds and to blame ourselves for the bad. We feel ashamed without knowing why. We submit to the kind of punishments we tolerated as children, and we offer ourselves no forgiveness. As parents sometimes do to kids, we neglect our bodies or judge them harshly. Refusing to take responsibility for the stories we tell, we blame the human body for our discomfort and pain. Then we go a step farther: we invent other characters to take the blame.

Having grown up believing in goblins and Santa Claus, we're used to the feeling of being watched and judged. We expect to be punished by someone for something. Why shouldn't we feel anxious and neurotic? We fear the wrath of whatever god we were taught to believe in. We want to appease angels and blame devils for the "awful" things we do. We watch ourselves in action, we condemn, and we punish. It seems we're willing to remain immature just to avoid taking charge of our reality.

By imagining ourselves as the central character in our life story, we add ourselves to a long list of childhood fictional creatures—except *me* seems to be the only one who isn't taking the blame. We say things like, "My bad" and "I have only myself to blame," but we're not talking about the mind—or about the main character of our story. We're almost always blaming the human body. We judge it, and we usually find it guilty.

When the main character acts like a big judge, our bodies react in fear. *Me* is the schoolyard bully in our world, ready to punch and intimidate. The main character of everyone's story is the rule maker, the judge, and the enforcer—and also the president of a very private nation. So we need to pay attention to the way we speak through *me*.

A forgiving mind is just and fair. Forgiveness creates immunities from pain. We don't have to punish ourselves for past mistakes or invent new mistakes out of our imagination. Whatever the circumstances, we are all doing our best. Tomorrow, we can do even better, but not if we're afraid of the one who is in charge of our judicial system—not if we're afraid of the judge. We all need checks and balances, which we can only exercise through self-awareness. We need to make sure our laws don't continue to harm the human being; we need to ensure that our reality is not being ruled by a lunatic.

How do lunatics behave? They disrespect the human body and punish it for their own bad choices. They lie to themselves. They take everything personally. They invent conflicts and enjoy the drama. They let self-importance make decisions for them. They let fear control them. Fighting over opinions is a little insane. Insisting on having the last word is exhausting. Putting conditions on love sounds self-defeating. Still, we do crazy things like that all the time. And we suffer for it.

It seems we make all kinds of excuses to suffer. Suffering is the only addiction for most of us, and we find many ways to create it. We want to be right at any cost and suffer when we're proven wrong. We suffer for our own judgments, and we continually imagine that we're being judged. We suffer for our bad habits—blaming cigarettes, drugs, or alcohol. We blame food. We blame sports. We blame everything on our upbringing. We blame loved ones for our unhappiness. And, of course, we blame the physical body for letting us down.

This may not be easy to admit—it may not seem easy to fix—but, with a little insight, we can make a corrupt system impeccable again. We can respect ourselves—for no reason and every reason. We can become our own champion and best friend, refusing to suffer—whatever the circumstance.

Why does any human suffer? The problem is almost always leadership. Reliable leaders take care of their country—their body—first. Aware leaders will not believe the lies they tell themselves. Effective leaders don't submit to fear or intimidation. The mind leads because we allow it to lead. We believe in the character it created and allow it to speak on our behalf. We believe its opinions and its recollections, but *me* does not represent the truth.

The mind cannot duplicate the truth. Truth is pure energy. Becoming aware of ourselves as energy, or truth, is an important revelation. The mind will continue to talk, sounding for all the world like a knowledgeable friend, but we don't have to believe it. We can rise above the voice of *me* at any time.

Me is the point of view of *life*'s reflection. It is an artificial intelligence. *Life*'s information is filtered through all the thoughts and characteristics we've given ourselves. The main character has its own intelligence, but every *me* is different, depending on the development of the brain and circumstances that affect the physical body. Each of us identifies with that character, so we find it difficult to separate *me* from reality.

So it follows that we allow *me* to rule, without any interference.

8

The Commander in Chief

By TRYING TO answer the question "Who am I?" you can begin to discern who you are not. You are not your body, but you are the guardian of its welfare and integrity. You are not the stories you tell about yourself. You are not the main character of those stories, but you believe you are—so completely that you are sometimes willing to defend its point of view with your life. You are not your mind, but you are responsible for the message it delivers to your body. You are also responsible for the message it delivers *through* your body to the rest of humanity.

Your mind has learned to operate like a government composed of three branches. It has a congress that makes up laws. A judicial branch enforces those laws through a system of rewards and punishments similar to the methods your family and community used to domesticate you. In this chapter we will cover the executive branch, and the "president" in charge of making decisions.

First, let's understand that the leader of your own nation is not real. The one who rules your little government is something out of your imagination but nevertheless has the power to affect your world.

So what kind of leader do you want to be? Remember, you can't give what you don't have. If you want to be more compassionate, you must treat yourself with compassion. If you want to represent the truth to others, stop lying to yourself. If you want to love someone in the truest sense, love yourself without conditions.

As with any government, the mind needs to make

decisions that serve the body. The mind's addictions become the body's addictions, and so we should all stop making excuses to suffer. Whether the physical body is healthy or sick, it needs a trustworthy caretaker. It can't flourish when it's being pushed beyond reason. It needs comfort, not criticism. It needs messages of delight, not doom. It needs to laugh.

Responsible leaders rule fairly. Wise commanders know the power they wield over other minds and hearts and they use that power carefully. They are aware of imbalances and prejudices within their administration. Without conscious leadership, the entire country suffers. Consider what kind of leader you are or want to be, and consider the people your leadership will affect on a daily basis.

If we want to preside over this body (our country) more wisely than we have been doing, we need to give our governing style a fair assessment. We need to be honest with ourselves, admit to our mistakes, and be willing to change. All three branches of government need to be accountable for the happiness of the human being. If we're unwilling to pay attention to our personal evolution, the body will continue to pay a price.

The main character of our story, *me*, wants to preside over everything. The problem, of course, is that *me* has long been a victim. *Me* feels persecuted by the system or judged by society. *Me* is forever on the defensive, and so how can *me* be a strong leader? How can *me* be an impartial judge?

In the same way, *me* could be perpetually angry or resentful. If *me* is constantly critical, how can it work harmoniously with other branches of government? If *me* is a judge and a bully, how can it achieve the wisdom necessary to guide a nation? How do informal agreements get made between leaders, and how do treaties get approved?

For many people, a victim has been acting as commander in chief of their country's armed forces. That puts the whole country at risk. What is a victim? Someone who complains all the time. Someone who sees personal injustice everywhere and insists on "being treated fairly." Clearly, there's nothing fair about one individual wanting the benefit of everyone's attention. There's no justice in a system ruled by one person's needs, with little concern for the needs of others.

When we think we're victimized, we become unreasonable. When we're insecure, small battles grow into major conflicts. When war breaks out, who pays the ultimate price? The body does—and it's hard to generate happiness again. We feel physically assaulted and dispirited, simply because of what we believe to be true.

Spirit means *life*, and *life* is the truth of what we are. We are spiritually mature when we are in a close relationship with *life*—when we can tell the real from the unreal. Wonderful relationships can't happen when we're obsessed with *me* and all things that concern *me*. Peace won't happen as long as we're waging wars within us and around us.

Our bodies feel the stress and anxiety we create by constantly being a victim or a judge. This makes it especially important to consider the way we lead— how we legislate, how we execute decisions, and how we choose our punishments. Our bodies feel the abuses first, but they aren't the only ones. How do we treat all the citizens of our nation—those who work with us, live with us, and depend on us? We can be an example of what bad governing does to good human beings—or we can show them what it takes to live functional, happy lives.

Physical development is built into our biological blueprint, but spiritual evolution needs our attention and our will. How the main character tells its story affects the mood of the country and its closest allies. Humans are social animals, and the mind mirrors our need for other bodies—in other words, it likes to connect with other minds. It sets up strongholds in other dreams by sending its best ambassadors— words and ideas. It sets up embassies in other people's realities, claiming a little bit of influence for itself.

Once we inhabit space in other people's minds, it's tempting to interfere in their business. We might question their culture, overlooking the fact that we're in their world, not ours. The positive effect we have on people is the result of our respect for their traditions and beliefs. Peace is the result of honoring the way other humans do things without imposing our laws on them.

We all want peace; we all want to feel that our world is safe. We want to feel secure, and we want to feel proud of ourselves. It's funny how we love to praise the country we live in, but have never learned to praise the body that serves as a home to us. Our physical body is an extension of who we are. It houses our mind. It is home to the infinite energy that runs through us. Are we proud of that? Are we willing to protect it, even above our favorite opinions?

When you travel, you may find that people of other cultures like to hear you describe your country. It feels good to tell them about its natural beauty and its many freedoms. Listen to what you tell people about your body as you go through an ordinary day. Do you talk about it with love and respect or with derision? What about its leadership? Does it inspire or intimidate? Is it sane, generous, and able to rise above its own story? Does it make people feel safe? How proud are you of the body that offers so many privileges?

The leader of your "country" is the one who is perceiving and describing everything. The one reading these words is the main character of your story. You are the president of your own nation, and you submit to all the rules you've put into place, based on what you've observed in your lifetime. You can see that you're the one who creates and enforces the rules, whether they seem fair or not. Your influence goes as far as your words go. Your command is as strong as your personal authority.

If you're able to see how your nation is run, you may also notice that everyone around you is the leader of their own nation. Your mother is a government of her own. Your father, your siblings, and your friends are ruled by their own governments.

You seek opportunities to participate in those governments. A government is influenced by the conversations of its people. The ideas that we send—by texting, talking, singing, or filming—go into other minds. Our ambassadors reach other nations, and we receive ambassadors from other nations. We all have influence on our governments, just as we have influence on our families, tribes, and cities. Together, we influence humanity—and the equilibrium of life on earth.

Being aware of that kind of power should encourage us to use it responsibly. Humans can't control the planet, but they can hurt it. As "president" we can't actually control the body we live in, but we can hurt it. We can't stop the body from getting old or sick, but we can injure it through our actions, reactions, and neglect. We can sedate it or intoxicate it. We can poison and corrupt it; and we do. Corruption, once again, is the problem. Truth is the solution.

What is truth? The truth cannot be explained with words. In fact, words take us farther from the truth, creating a reality of their own. However, we all know instinctively that there is more to us than words and theories. We were whole before we learned a language. We can feel whole again without relying on symbols to speak for us. Words are our emissaries, but, again, they are not the truth of us.

Close your eyes, and you can feel energy moving through you. You can feel it running under your skin, making it warm. Notice your breath, your heartbeat, your flickering eyelids. Move your fingers, your legs, your head, and feel the power that commands every motion. That power is *life*, flowing into all the little universes of you. Every emotion is real. Every sensory perception is telling you the truth. The thoughts that manipulate your emotions are not real.

What you are is pure energy, the force of *life*. Nothing else is real. The mind is a mirror reflection of the truth, and mirrors merely attempt to represent what is real. The reflection is only as good as the quality of the mirror. *Life*'s energy is real. It is what you are—what we all are. We don't have to prove our worth. We forget that, thinking we have to fight for recognition, and then fight to maintain it. We fight for attention. We fight over ideas and personal opinions at the expense of our emotional health. We fight to understand ourselves, and we fight to be understood.

Life is truth, and it doesn't need to be understood. Truth doesn't need proof, or even faith, to survive.

And it doesn't need our stories. Truth existed before stories, before humanity; and truth will continue after all the storytellers are gone. We don't need a thought or a theory to show us the truth. Truth can be felt in our loving and in our enduring passion to live.

If we understand how we govern ourselves, we can create a more benevolent government. We can change the temperament of its leader. Most of us are intimidated by power but eager to use power against ourselves. We can see violence everywhere, but not the kind of violence we inflict on our own bodies. We've tortured it to make it thinner, stronger, or more attractive. We've been unkind to the body, often trying to control its natural impulses. Seeing that, we can change. The human body has served us loyally, and it deserves loyalty in return.

We imagine that *life* looks upon us favorably or treats us badly, but *life* is what we are. Our minds can imagine so many things, so imagine how the mind can conspire with *life*. Imagine giving up control in this moment and surrendering to *life*. Imagine going through a day without having to be *me*. Using a little bit of imagination, we can govern ourselves in new ways and come up with solutions to recurring problems. After all, imagining and problem solving are what the mind does best.

We're all in the process of creating the reality we think we deserve, and each of us has defined the central character. Each of us sees the world through the eyes of *me*, and *me* is on autopilot, making rules and executing them without full awareness. Like all great stories, your personal story could use a hero. Your body could use a savior.

As it happens, the only one who can save you is the main character of your story. The one you call *me* is not real, but it affects real things. Rather than perceiving the truth, most of us yield to an inner voice. We listen to our own thoughts. We believe them and obey them, at the expense of our happiness. We focus on past conversations, past moments, past years. It may have taken time and patience to learn those habits, but they can be undone with far less effort. We have the tools. We have attention, memory, and imagination to guide us forward.

If *me* is the problem, *me* is also the solution. Your country already has a leader who wants to be wise and compassionate. If you're asking life's deeper questions, you may already be a president who's prepared to put the welfare of the country first. You have a legislature that wants to revise its laws, and a justice system that respects all individuals. You can sense what is real and what is not. You're ready to take the next step.

Change requires action. One action leads to another, and another, until new habits become automatic and changes become evident. In time, people's reactions change, and they see you differently. There's no need to look to other governments for solutions. You have all you need to build a healthy and prosperous nation. You have the will, and you have the awareness.

So if what we call reality is virtual and *me* is not real, then what about the world around us? What else isn't actually real?

What other pearls of wisdom have we overlooked?

Ask Yourself, "What Is Real?"

9

The Second Pearl

*What is real? You will know what is real
when you accept what is not real.*

ONCE WE LEARN to challenge our stories, we get a
sense of who we're not. Seeing that, we can become
aware of the truth. We can see everything from an
infinite point of view. You've grown accustomed to
seeing yourself as a product of life and perhaps even
as a victim of circumstance. By shifting your atten-

tion, you can see from another perspective: you are the artist of this creation. You are energy itself.

By asking the question "What is real?" we're challenging what we think we know. Nothing is quite as we imagine it. Again, think of the brain as a mirror. If our hands reached for an image in a mirror, we would touch glass, not the thing whose image it reflects. The mind uses information received by the brain to create a picture of reality. Thought is the reflection. If we tried to physically reach for a thought, we couldn't.

We look in a glass mirror to get an idea of how our bodies look. We depend on an accurate reflection, but we always get some degree of distortion. The mind reflects the truth in its particular way. It sees through the filter of existing ideas and opinions. It sees what it has been taught to expect. To one degree or another, we're all perceiving warped reflections of the truth.

Why is this important? Because, as we discovered earlier, we identify ourselves with the mind. We're totally convinced we are the main character in the mind's reality. Imagine what would happen if the reflection became aware of itself? This would probably create a huge disturbance. What if you realized you weren't your thoughts and beliefs—that you weren't even *me*?

It may not be easy to imagine; it may not seem like fun. Maybe you find just talking about minds, mirrors, and reflections disturbing. That's a good sign. It means you've just challenged a belief of some kind. You can deny the disturbance, of course, or you can recognize it—and even take advantage of it.

If you acknowledge that your mind is a mirror reflection of what is real, and not a very accurate one, you can see that yours is only one interpretation of reality—one of more than seven billion individual interpretations. Then you can experiment. You can put what the reflection is telling you in a reasonable perspective and move your attention to your senses. You can begin to notice how your body feels, emotionally and physically. Are those feelings coming from a memory? Are they reacting to an ongoing narrative? What are you telling yourself, and why?

When you're not thinking, your body is free to feel, without your interference. It will regulate emotional moods on its own. It will be able to tell you when something is physically wrong, and you will notice. You will be able to modify your habitual responses—like anger, indignation, and fear. Emotions will inform you, which is what emotions are supposed to do. No emotion should become addictive or chronic and sicken you.

Imagine it, and it can happen. Imagine finding emotional balance automatically. Imagine checking your thoughts all the time, no matter what is going on around you. It sounds funny, but by not thinking so much, you'll bring yourself closer to answering the question "What is real?" By perceiving without thinking, you'll notice what isn't real now and never was.

Pure perception is not about what you tell yourself. It doesn't rely on what other people tell you. Stop thinking—and you're able to observe, listen, and feel. The truth is obvious in everything you see and experience. Be still for a moment. Can you hear the voice of *me* commenting on this moment? It might be explaining what you're reading right now or planning what to do when you stop reading. It might be distracting itself, making comments about someone else—what she did, what he said. Maybe it's enjoying conversations that haven't happened and are unlikely ever to happen.

Your thoughts follow a story line, often with a beginning, a middle, and an end. The story includes familiar characters, most of whom you think you know well. Your reality is populated by other characters—not so much by actual people, but the things you think you know about those people. Events happen, and the people exist, but your understanding of them is the stuff of dreams. We're all "dreaming" reality.

When we're awake, our dream is typically based on real events, but we each interpret events differently. We see and hear things according to our particular beliefs and assumptions. As we've seen, everyone believes the "president" no matter what he or she is saying—and we all obey laws that exist within our personal reality.

Asleep, we're still dreaming, but the laws are different, if laws exist at all. The law of gravity may not exist in our sleeping dreams. The laws of physics are ignored, and basic logic becomes irrelevant. Our waking dream follows physical laws—and social and civic laws—but sleeping dreams happily ignore them. Either way, we're dreaming. We are all making distinct and separate impressions of this moment, wherever we are and whatever we're doing. The moment is real, but we're telling our own story about it. This is the wonderful magic of the human mind, to turn real things into symbols and impressions. But we shouldn't forget that the body responds emotionally to our kind of magic.

The waking dream can be mastered, just as we can alter the course of our nighttime dreaming. We can remind ourselves before falling asleep to wake up in the middle of a recurring nightmare. We can leave clues—to pinch ourselves or to challenge threatening characters in a sleeping dream. The same is true of our waking life. It's simple enough to remind ourselves that we're dreaming all the time, even as we go through an ordinary day. Other people are dreaming too, and their reality is based on what they think is true. It has nothing to do with us, unless we agree that it does.

Everyone has the power to steer their reality in a new direction. Everyone has a chance to alter its message. We created the idea of ourselves by listening to the opinions of people closest to us. They told us their version of who we are. We can't change the way other people perceive us, and it's not important to try. We can, however, take charge of our own dream.

At any point, we can modify the reflection so that it will better reflect the truth. We can stop assuming we know better than anyone else and start to ask questions. We can stop insisting that we're right. It's not a sign of weakness to surrender the need to know. We can even question our own knowledge. We can disregard our own advice and trust *life* more. We alter the face of *me*. By adopting energy's point of view, we let go of our small obsessions. By seeing beyond our own concerns, we can appreciate the infinite landscape.

Each of us is pure energy, caught up in the dream of matter. We assume we know who we are. We assume we can discern what is real. We believe all our assumptions are true—until we start to doubt. That's the first step in answering "What is real?" Our sense of reality starts to shift when we question what we believe.

10

Life Under Tyranny

THERE IS ONLY one truth: energy. Energy is the force that creates and sustains the universe. We use different words for it: *life,* truth, intent, love. They all point to the same thing. Energy is *life.* Matter is a copy of *life.* It is a copy of truth. The mind is a reflection of that truth—and, like that painting we mentioned, it offers many clues about the artist.

Our impression of reality is changing constantly. In that sense, there's no solid ground under our feet.

Reality isn't what we imagine it is in this moment. In fact, reality isn't what it seemed to be a minute ago. It will be something else a minute from now, an hour from now—and it won't stop changing. We'd like to think it's fixed, solid. We'd like our impression of reality to be everyone's impression. We like to feel safe, knowing that the world is what we think it is—but impressions change, don't they? Everything is shifting, transforming, whether or not we notice.

The main character is also shifting constantly. It all started when we were toddlers, learning to speak and then to think. Thinking is the act of talking to ourselves. We mimicked other characters, saying what they said and thinking what they thought, until we felt confident to narrate our own dream. The *me* that we first imagined wasn't the *me* that went to kindergarten, learning to interact with other *me*'s. *Me* isn't what it was then, or what it became in college, or what it was when we first got married. The *me* who is now a parent can hardly remember the *me* who was single.

The person we think we are has changed over the years, as we accumulated experiences and processed new information. It has acted selfishly and generously. It has been reckless, and it has been responsible. It has been an unreliable caretaker for the physical body as well as a devoted one. The characteristics of *me* are changing constantly. As *me* changes, so does its impression of reality.

Every human sees reality a little differently—or a lot differently—from every other. Reality changes with our changing circumstances. Reality looks different according to where we're sitting, standing, or walking. If we take one step in any direction, our view of the world changes—instantly, we can see things that weren't apparent before. If we lie down or stand on a ladder, we've changed our point of view of things. If we're riding a bike or driving a car, scenes fly by at different speeds. What we call reality is more of a moving-picture show.

Change the country, language, or culture, and our sense of reality gets a shock. Nothing smells the same or sounds the same. No one talks like us. Our smallest routines are disrupted. People everywhere find ways to feed and shelter themselves, but their ways are distinct. They raise children and provide for their families, but the rules change with the scenery—reality's landscape is constantly evolving. If we're okay with this, we can start to wake up and pay attention.

If we experience a traumatic event, we get jolted out of our normal perceptions and the world is suddenly not the same—it may never be the same. A car accident or the loss of a loved one makes existence feel threatening and unpredictable. In a crisis, the mind stops its narrative and isn't sure how to pick it up again. Time slows, speeds up, or becomes irrelevant. Why does tragedy have this effect on us? Tragedy creates changes that seem too big for the mind to accept. It struggles to put the old *me* into the context of a new reality. For a mind that hasn't learned to be a friend and ally to the body, the struggle usually ends in failure. We feel heartbroken and abandoned by life.

The mind is an ally when it adapts to abrupt changes, whether those changes are tragic or gratifying. Our existence includes all events and all possibilities. Every experience is an integral part of being alive. All emotions are acceptable. We don't need to play a role or act out our feelings for dramatic effect. We don't need to follow the mind's programming, responding to events the way we were taught to respond. We don't have to follow old laws. At any time, in any situation, we can experience events from the perspective of *life* itself.

The law of *life*, we can say, is to create and never stop creating. Transformation is *life*'s chief characteristic. *Life* has no *me*. It doesn't feel victimized and never casts blame. In the infinite picture, there is no judge; *life* makes no judgments. From *life*'s point of view, there are no crimes or penalties—only transformations. Energy transforms, but never stops. It is everywhere, it is infinite, and it is eternal. We know that, but we don't know ourselves as energy. We see ourselves as separate from it, and consequently separate from truth.

We live in a world of rules and rarely gaze beyond that world. Those rules become irrelevant when we sleep, but fall back into place as soon as the mind wakes up—almost as soon. There's a moment, before we open our eyes, when we're not sure where we are—or who we are. The moment passes quickly, because we've learned to "reconstruct" ourselves automatically. We've done this so many times we don't notice the process. We open our eyes, and we remember: "I'm at home," or, "I'm still in a hotel . . . um, in Denver, I think. . . . No, it's Monday, so I'm in Dayton."

Having established where we are, we put together the pieces of *who* we are—and there are many, many little pieces. Again, the process is automatic and barely noticeable. We remember who we went to bed with and roll over to make sure. We remember what we were worried about when we went to sleep the night before—and begin to worry again. We remind ourselves what reality we're living in and start the dream all over again.

If we slowed the process down, it would probably be like reading a fairy tale to a child, sounding something like this: "And then he remembered he was Timmy, who fell asleep under a willow tree after running away from his home, which stood on the edge of a village called . . ." We put our personal story together in a fraction of a second, get the appropriate emotions on board, and then *me* is ready to face the day.

If our sense of reality hasn't undergone any recent disruptions, most of us settle into a familiar pattern of thought and behavior. Of course, these are patterns that have been constrained by laws—our laws. Like little kids expecting to be bullied at school, we wake up most days with a vague sense of guilt. We've probably messed up somehow and can only hope that we don't get caught. We hope we're not exposed as liars or pretenders. We hope we're not going to be judged or contradicted, and then we step out of the house, armed with our best stories.

With all our defenses, we still won't avoid conflict. We will surely clash with other opinions and offend other feelings. The best of us get defensive and even aggressive on occasion. Even the most even-tempered person can get provoked. Even the most honorable president acts unwisely now and then. We govern our world poorly sometimes, disappointing ourselves and the people we care about. Sometimes, we may inadvertently start a war.

As long as the war continues in our own heads, our relationships with others will be compromised. When we fail to get along with ourselves, our efforts to get along with other people will be frustrated. Our internal private tyrannies grow into public tyrannies, and soon family members are fighting, friends fall out, and entire communities are in conflict. Everyone needs to be right. Everyone is yelling, and no one is listening.

Listening is essential. We need to listen to ourselves first. It's important to learn our mind's particular language. Even silently, it uses words to accuse and to demoralize the body, words it learned long ago. "What an idiot!" we say to ourselves. "I'm such a dummy," "I'm hideous," "I'm a freak!" Are we listening to this? The disrespect is clear, and it will be reflected in the way other people speak to us.

If we listen, we can change the way we communicate with ourselves. We can base even this relationship on respect. Where is the compassion we're naturally inclined to give a friend, a child, or a favorite pet? It's there, of course, but we never learned to treat our own bodies as well as we would a pet dog or cat. We can just as easily choose to say things to ourselves like, "Come on, you're amazing, but right now you're just tired." We can follow a curse with an apology, telling the body we're sorry for the insult. We can laugh at ourselves with affection.

It's not so hard to learn the language of respect. We can be patient with our blunders. "Man, I really love you!" we can say out loud. "Silly thing! You crack me up!" is a fair response to an ordinary mistake. If we're fair to ourselves, we will judge the world fairly. If we keep our inner dialogue honest, we can build trust between mind and body—the most important relationship there is.

As you've begun to see, we rule ourselves in ways we don't notice. The body notices, however, and responds to our tyrannies the way it would respond to physical threats. It responds to toxic thoughts the way it might respond to a virus. It fights the invasion and often loses—even if we don't notice. Self-judgment is an assault, and so is self-contempt. It's an attack on the body to pity ourselves, to worry, or to obsess.

The most amazing thing about the body is that it recovers from most abuses on its own. Cuts heal; broken bones mend. Diseases are attacked and defeated. When our planet changes temperature, it makes chemical adjustments and stabilizes. Our bodies do the same. However, if the assaults to the body are constant and long overlooked, the damage may become irreversible.

Our attitudes about ourselves strike us physically, and so we need to play a different role. Each of us needs to be the peacekeeper, not the tyrant. We want to be conscious guardians of freedom for the human body we occupy. We are adults now, whose parents and siblings should no longer run our lives. Many of us are parents now or even grandparents. We're in charge of our actions and our reactions. We're capable leaders in our own right.

Then why do we insist on waging internal wars? Why do we build prisons for ourselves and make our bodies live within them? Why do we insist that other people must suffer with us? When we feel badly treated, we fight back. When our notions of reality are rigid, we feel trapped. Of course, we feel like running away. Naturally, we want to know what real freedom feels like. So what's stopping us?

11

Getting Out of Jail

WE ALL REMEMBER what it was like to be a teenager, sick of the indignities of childhood. We wanted to break away from our parents. We wanted to escape the prison of home and family. Some of you reading this may still be teenagers, but even in adulthood most people have the impulse to break free of something. Even in old age, we want to exercise our independence. This impulse to be free is natural, but who is really standing in our way?

No matter how unfair outside circumstances seem, feelings of oppression begin with us. We entertain some unpleasant ideas about ourselves. We hang on to irrational fears and create random superstitions. We tell ourselves we can't, we shouldn't—or else. We demand some kind of penance for having too much fun. We punish ourselves for breaking unwritten rules. We even make ourselves pay penalties for loving.

Oppression exists. There are real prisoners in the world and actual prisons, but most people are oppressed by their own stories and fears. They're driven to despair by beliefs they refuse to abandon. They are nagged by voices only they can hear. No one can say what it is you demand of yourself except you. No one thinks about ways to punish you but you. So listen to yourself. Hear how you tell people you don't do that or eat that or how you're not that kind of guy. Listen to your thoughts, and hear how you browbeat yourself. You may sound like your father sometimes, or your mother, or your college math professor. Mostly, you sound like that character you invented to keep yourself in line. You sound like *me*.

A strong desire for freedom usually begins in adolescence. All kids, at some time or another, begin to feel constrained and a little persecuted. Parents try to shape and protect their children, but kids reach a point when they resent them for it. They rebel, even if it means hurting themselves in the process. Society gets involved, but kids lose patience with its rules. Governments and religious institutions want to lead them in one direction or another. Breaking free of it all sounds appealing, but most people want freedom to be given to them. That won't happen. The freedom that really counts is the freedom we grant ourselves.

Tyranny starts with us and with that little government in our heads. Who makes the rules? Who enforces them? Who can rewrite those rules? The president can—the aware executive we want to be. We can each repeal our own laws and reform our own personal justice system. We can break out of jail free anytime.

As you've probably figured out by now, *me* can become a better decision maker. *Me* can be a better administrator—or *me* can step aside and become a friend. If the desire is there, *me* can be a diplomat and a peacemaker. *Me* can ultimately be the savior you've been looking for.

12

The Diplomat

As we described earlier, humanity first organizes itself into families, then communities and cities, then states, and finally into countries and kingdoms. Each country has borders to keep out foreign intruders. Around the globe, there are hundreds of languages spoken, making communication even more challenging. But countries need to communicate with each other. People need to gather and share ideas. They need to listen, without judgment.

Every country needs diplomats to do the job of reaching out and connecting with other countries. Every nation needs people who are skilled communicators and negotiators. Every human body could use an ally.

What kind of mind is an ally to the human body? It's a mind that listens to itself and rejects thought-stories of hate. "I hate myself!" is an example of unskilled communication. Who is hating what? Are you hating your body or your circumstances? Are you dissatisfied with the effect you seem to have on other people? "I hate you!" usually means someone in your life isn't obeying you. We can't control most people, and we shouldn't want to. Chances are, they've practiced being their own kind of tyrant, strictly controlling themselves and managing everyone around them, just like you.

An ally doesn't gossip or judge—the kind of things that are toxic to the body. So many of our thoughts are self-degrading, and so many of our commentaries make us suspicious and afraid of other people. "Carla is such a snob," or "Jimmy is such a jerk," may have sounded cool in high school, but where does it get us now? It gets us into the habit of complaining, for one. How can the body be happy and confident in an environment of prejudice and disgust? Judgments blind us to people's truth and push away our friends. Who can trust someone who judges everything so harshly? How can we even trust ourselves?

Most of us didn't start life this way. We were born into families that spoke to us kindly. When we finally began to speak, we spoke like them. We soon found out that words brought us what we needed. Growing up with many people under the same roof, we learned to use words effectively to make our desires known. To keep the peace, we had to listen to other points of view. In school, our ability to use words got us good grades and made us new friends. College and the bigger world helped us refine those skills, as we learned to negotiate, to charm, to build trust, and more. We learned the art of diplomacy.

With a little diplomacy, we found we could fit

into most social circles. Learning how to be diplomatic made it easier to get employment and to stay in positions of influence. We discovered that tact and sensitivity could bridge differences between people and resolve conflicts. Respect for others—and for other realities—could save us.

At some point, we all had to learn the language of our profession. Every business has its terms and code phrases, and every workplace has a government of its own. Every generation uses its own idioms, and every region has its own dialect. People around the globe speak the language of their peers, their vocation, their fellow citizens, their culture.

We are all members of a species that needs to communicate with words in order to survive. Good communication takes a willingness to recognize common interests and to make alliances. People are at their best when they feel they can trust each other to listen, to agree, and to honor agreements. If we refuse to talk, how can we avoid hostilities? If we have no respect for other cultures, how can we excel as humans?

It's in our nature to cooperate, and history tells us that peaceful coexistence is in the best interest of our species. And yet rulers sometimes invent conflicts. Leaders want more power. Nations overtake nations. We see how the world of politics works, but what about the world within us? How can we make things better in our own dream?

Our body wants the company of other bodies, but our mind—our internal government—often has a different agenda. To avoid continuing conflicts within us, we need to use our diplomatic skills for a different purpose. The mind needs to make a treaty with the physical body it occupies. It needs to make new agreements, and it needs to honor those agreements. Mind and body need to sit down and talk.

"I promise I won't hurt you" sounds odd at first, but it's an important message to give the body. "I've put my self-importance above your needs, but I want to do better. I want to be a friend, not a tyrant." Say something like that a few times, and you'll begin to recognize your neglect and abuses. You'll listen to your thoughts. You'll become a little more honest with yourself. You'll connect with something you've taken for granted most of your life—your human body. Turn your attention to this relationship. Talk out loud more often, so that you can recognize repetitive words and attitudes. With patience, you'll begin to modify the voice in your head.

The body can do its part in mending the relationship too. It needs to learn to wait before responding emotionally to everything you say. Give it permission to ignore your chatter. Give it a break from *me*. It will soon adapt to a style of leadership that shows restraint and good timing. The human body was meant to communicate effectively with *life*, even as events change and shift. As you achieve more awareness, you can allow that kind of communication. You don't need to interfere. As a result, your body will be less intimidated by management— and, with practice, it will be the equal partner it was meant to be.

When the relationship between *me* and the body works well, all our relationships improve. We become more generous, without trying. We don't have to play roles. We don't have to twist ourselves into shapes to please other people. We don't need lies or alibis. Authenticity will carry us through each moment and all moments.

We are *life*, creating new dreams and remarkable beauty everywhere we go. We are also the emissaries of *life*, mending divisions and connecting people. The best leaders are plain-speaking communicators. They say what they mean and mean what they say. We all have the ability to be clear and honest with ourselves. We don't need to accumulate any more superstitions, and we can eliminate the ones we have. Awareness and authenticity are a natural result of having a mind that respectfully communicates with the body, so the body can better commune with *life*.

And what about getting along with other bodies, with other minds? Like all foreign relations, it helps to learn a language that their governments understand. By listening to others, we get a sense of how their realities work and who is in charge. It allows us to speak directly to them, rather than the people we would prefer them to be. When we were growing up, the unspoken message we got from our caretakers was, "Be like me." Has that become your message to the people around you? You can be a better diplomat in the world at large, but you need to start by shedding the habits that made you guarded, suspicious, and untrue to yourself. Your mind dispatches all communications. How is it representing the truth, right now?

The language that the mind speaks to the body is the language we speak to everyone we meet. Your words can be impeccable ambassadors, representing truth and intent, starting with the words you think. You give them that authority; no one else can. They have no meaning, no authority of their own. You determine whether words—even a word like *me*—serve your body or disparage it. You choose the phrases and ideas that shape your personal reality. At any time, you can decide whether they are serving *life*.

Language is driven by our intent—the power of our will. Language can create a masterpiece out of the most modest dream. Ideas create a heaven for us to live in, or they keep us in hell. How do you communicate with yourself? Are you in the habit of delivering messages of outrage or fear? Do you invent excuses to be defensive? How does your body feel about that? When toxic messages are spoken out loud and often, we eventually crave the emotional results—fury, disappointment, alarm. By repeating messages of appreciation for ourselves and others, we develop an appetite for respect.

Respect is the solution to humanity's problems, from global unrest, to playground scuffles, to the delicate balance of power that exists in our own minds. Respect opens the door to cooperation and understanding in any culture. Respect means we honor everyone's right to exist. Respect is the best part of love.

Every one of us creates the kind of reality we think we deserve, but our human body deserves far more than we've given it. It deserves, above all, the happiness that comes from a sane and peaceful mind.

13

Peace and Sanity

A GOVERNMENT IS swayed by the mood of its citizens. Humanity as a whole is guided by the balance and composure of each of its members. Every person is an essential part of the body of humanity, and so your personal evolution counts. It matters. How people rule themselves privately extends outward. How we rule ourselves is reflected in the way we are ruled. This is how the human dream works, and it changes by the will of each human, with time and practice.

Our personal dream can change whenever we say so. Sure, it may take a little effort, but not as much as it took to become our own petty tyrants. *Me* began when we first learned to talk and has consumed our attention ever since. Most of us can't imagine ourselves without a main character. We find it difficult to imagine a moment or two without our own voice chattering in our heads. Most of us think we'll never be free of our relentless thinking, which is a problem; but solving problems is the mind's special talent. By giving some attention to our inner narrative as we go through the day, we can make real changes. Thoughts will respond. Words will obey. By directing our efforts toward mental peace and calm, we can rise above the noise.

We all know that it's not enough that other people want us to change. We have to want it too. Desire is a motivating force, a way to direct energy consciously. We often think we have to wait for desire to come to us; we think we have to be in the mood before we act. If we always waited for the right mood, nothing would change.

Action is vital to our own evolution, as it is to *life*. We need to keep growing, changing, and challenging our beliefs. If reality was a car, desire would be the gas pedal. Step on it, and the car moves. Press harder, and it moves faster. Desire generates and directs energy; it's ours to play with. If we're not feeling the desire, then we can summon it. Whatever spiritual teachings say about desire, it fuels our actions—for our own good or ill. Desire moves us in one of two directions, and it's important to understand the difference.

Ideally, desire moves us toward passion, the power of love. Loving what we do leads to inspiration. Events won't always yield to our desires, but if obstacles slow us down, we can change course. We can redirect our energies without resentment or frustration. It does no good to push against other people's wishes or to find fault with other realities. We can move forward in other ways, and new directions bring unexpected opportunities.

Desire guides our passion and inspiration; inspiration leads to creativity. Desire can also drive us over a cliff—it can lead to obsession. Putting the full power of attention on one object of desire makes us fanatical—meaning we want something so much that we can't see anything else. This goes way beyond a passion for football or a love for punk rock. Who hasn't been enthralled by an idea, a philosophy, or a person? In time, nothing else matters. We could be desperately hooked on drugs or alcohol, ignoring countless warnings and offers to help. However we become fixated, we risk losing touch with the ones who love us—and our own power is squandered and misused.

How do we tell whether our desires are inspired or obsessive? Inspiration leads us to create new things and new realities; obsession leads to many types of destruction. When we're obsessed, we can't see clearly and we can't react freely. We may starve a good relationship or ruin a promising career. We compromise our physical health and sanity. Soon enough, obsession will devastate our world and many of the people in it.

It's easy to become fanatical without knowing it.

We can mistake it for healthy enthusiasm, until we look around and realize how much was lost while our attention was diverted. Our desires can take us into dangerous terrain, but desire can also bring us back to peace and sanity. Desire pushes humans toward greatness and creativity. Passion inspires ideas and innovations; it stirs the flames of romance and seals lifelong unions.

We're talking about getting back to sanity—so does that mean we're insane? Well, sure. Each of us knows how irrational we can get sometimes, so let's be as honest as we can. Let's look at some of the things we do. We believe almost everything we hear and everything we think. We can rarely tell the difference between real and unreal. We walk through a world of living things and actual people, but respond primarily to a virtual one. We let thoughts guide feelings. We judge, but we're unwilling to be judged. We take everything personally, as if only *me* exists. We build hierarchies of importance—ranking some humans at the top and some at the bottom. We want love, but we use love as a weapon against ourselves. If we're even willing to show contempt for the body that made all our dreaming possible—we must be crazy.

When we wake up and see things as they are, it feels like being sober at a party full of drunks. Imagine being at a big boisterous affair, where all the guests have been drinking for a long time. Their actions are senseless. Their words are reckless. Gossip starts, and the poison spreads quickly. We could say all of humanity is at this party—where rumors run wild, feelings get hurt, and reactions get violent. The spectacle is a strange one if you're not drinking.

If we're not drunk, we have the advantage of seeing what's happening around us. We see how everyone is intoxicated, and they think the other guests don't notice. At an actual party, the level of chaos depends on how much alcohol people have consumed. In this metaphorical party, the degree of insanity depends on how much false information people accept and absorb. It depends on how superstitious they are and how much they lie to themselves.

Superstitions are beliefs that have authority over our thinking. We give them that authority, of course. If we put faith in an idea, it will determine the way we think and behave. This isn't just about worshipping or believing in old wives' tales. Most people's superstitions are more subtle than that. Believing that words have power over you is a superstition— words have no power except the power you give them. It's superstitious to believe in all the little lies you tell yourself. It's superstitious to believe that life is rewarding you for good behavior and punishing you for breaking rules, just the way your parents did. It's superstitious to think that truth can be lost or destroyed. It's superstitious to imagine that truth is somewhere outside of you, unreachable and mysterious.

Most of humanity is driving under the influence of one superstition or another. We may still believe what our parents have been telling us since infancy. We believe what our ancestors believed. We believe what everyone else believes. Most of all, we believe ourselves.

Humans are thinkers, philosophers, and they use language to communicate ideas. They use sounds and symbols to inform themselves and to teach each other. We are all scientists, searching for the truth. Of course, we usually settle for a best guess based on the information available to us. We give power to our assumptions and let fear control and even intoxicate us.

Throughout our time on earth, we've looked at the stars to predict the future. Until recently, humans were nearly helpless at night, depending on the moon's light. Without it, we were unable hunt, to travel, or to do battle. An eclipse might have signaled the end of the world. Any disturbance in nature might have seemed like punishment from the heavens. In our fear, we concluded that the gods were laughing at us or that demons controlled the earth and sky. Earthquakes were a sign of one god's wrath; floods were a sign of another god's indifference. Ending a drought required a sacrifice; rain required a feast. Fear works like a virus in the human dream. We contract each other's fears and make them our own. We give power to ideas. We catch cultural viruses, and we spread them.

When we're sober and sane, the effect of superstition on humanity is obvious. We see how one person can make a suggestion, and people react as if it were truth. We see how contagious ideas can be. An adept communicator can sway a crowd. One person, reacting in anger and making a case for fear, will inspire a thousand others to follow. One cries, "Fire!" and a hundred others will panic. Superstitions corrupt human imagination. Without superstition, imagination can bring great visions into being. Imagination encourages evolution, but it needs to be kept safe from the influences of fear.

It's not so hard to wake up and be sane. The folly can end with us—one dreamer at a time. Each of us can sober up and observe the party of revelers. We can see how many people deliberately choose to stay drunk. We can see how much poison they're willing to tolerate and ask ourselves, "Is that how I want to live my life? Am I really so afraid to be conscious and fully aware?" We can see how drunk

we've become and say no to common fears and superstitions. We can end our addiction to worry and
to drama.

Wake up, open your eyes, and see life in front
of you—and everywhere. Use your attention, your
brain's most remarkable power, to see the truth in
people. See beyond the drunkards, with all their
opinions and phobias—even if one of those drunkards is you. Maybe you're the drama queen, the
critic, or the cynic. See beyond your own stories—
your thoughts and your assumptions. Instead of se-
dating yourself to keep from hearing the noise, *listen*.
Pay attention. Observe. Say no to the thoughts that
make you crazy. Say no to a runaway narrative. The
storyteller is someone you invented, accustomed to
saying the same old things the same old way. Say no
to that voice in your head.

See fear for what it typically is: the body's response
to *me*. Most of us spend our lives running from our
own voice. We run from our thoughts because we
believe them. They scare us, they defame us, and still
we believe them. Use your senses, and bypass think-

ing altogether. Play with *life*, the way you used to before there was a government operating in you—back
before there were laws, penalties, and a president to
answer to. Quiet down, and open up emotionally.
Let *life* play with you.

Then you might be ready to accept the truth
about love.

ASK YOURSELF, "WHAT IS LOVE?"

14

The Third Pearl

*What is love? You will know love when
you realize what love is not.*

YOU CAN'T FULLY understand yourself until you're
able to identify yourself as *life*—as energy's eternal
force. How does that awareness help you? It puts
all your efforts into perspective. It makes knowledge
your servant, not your master. It makes your virtual
reality a playful work of art, not a prison. It changes

the voice of *me*, making it possible to transcend the main character.

Me doesn't need to be defeated or replaced. Through you, it can evolve. The evolution of *me* is a choice. You decide how you feel about yourself from moment to moment. By shifting your attention just a little, you've been getting an idea of what you're not. You've asked, "What is real?" and begun the process of doubting what you think you know. This process goes on, deepens, and will lead to greater discoveries—but the truth is simple. Truth is *life*; it is not a system of beliefs. Truth is infinite and everlasting, but your body and your dream are not. Truth is energy, power. Truth is the reality of you.

We can also say that truth is love.

What most of us call love is the opposite of love. Our problems exist because we are taught to love with conditions. This is not just our personal problem; it's humanity's problem. No matter the culture, we are taught to corrupt love. We are taught to distrust the only real thing there is: *life*'s infinite force.

Rules and conditions have defined the way we love. As we've seen, people build their own governments with self-made laws and penalties. We take our laws seriously, and we're strict about their execution. None of this is right or wrong; it's a fact. Domestication shaped our behaviors. We were judged and disciplined as children and, as adults, we learned to judge and to discipline ourselves. We punish ourselves and we pardon ourselves, but what exactly is our crime?

The biggest crimes are the ones we commit against our own body. If you are the kind of tyrant who insults your body, it's likely that you'll treat other bodies with disrespect. If you're inclined to hurt yourself physically, you'll probably feel okay about hurting others. Either way, your body will pay the price.

Hurting other people comes back to us in one way or another. Judging or abusing people will lead to punishments even we can't regulate. We will be treated in the same way we treat other humans. If society judges us and finds us guilty, we're punished. And again, the body suffers. Whatever our abuses, the human body pays.

When we berate ourselves, the body pays an emotional price. And we do berate ourselves, of course.
Most of us, at one time or another, have watched
people marching down a city sidewalk muttering to
themselves. We've seen people so possessed by anger
that they're yelling and screaming at no one. Are we
so different?

We frequently yell and scream at ourselves, but silently. We walk down the street complaining to ourselves, reviewing old conversations, and making up
new ones. Our lips are moving, and our faces show
the strain. We could be on the phone, but aren't we
just using someone else as an excuse to rant? When
the voice in our head becomes unbearable to us, it
shouts out for the world to hear. The thing is, no
one really wants to hear it, and no one wants to witness the battles being waged inside of us.

A phone to our ear may make us appear less crazy,
and it may help us feel less alone; but we don't need
the phone or the friend. If we feel miserable at times,
it's probably because we're believing something that's
not true. We're hearing our own voice scolding us.

When it does, we're children again, afraid and be-wildered. We're teenagers again, knowing for sure we'll be grounded. We're drunk drivers, about to be pulled over and fined. The voice is ours, however it sounds, and we can stop it.

The voice of *me* has been running the show for so long we hardly notice. Once we notice, we can save ourselves. We can regain a little sanity. At any time, we can politely end the conversation we're hav-ing with ourselves. Just as we do when we're on the phone, we can say we have to go. "I gotta run, honey. All my love. Bye-bye." We can do this any time— while driving, on the street, or even while trying to go to sleep at night. "Ciao. Gotta go," and we hang up on ourselves.

Nothing improves by continuing the conversation. An appetite for poison will lead to more poison. No problem is ever solved by rebuking ourselves or blaming someone else. We have to put an end to our own bullying. The conversations we have with our-selves aren't real, but they create real emotions in us and real turmoil in our lives.

Emotions aren't the problem. Our thoughts are. Emotions tell us the truth about what's going on inside of us. When we feel anger, our pulse quickens, our breathing becomes erratic, and our muscles tense. Our thoughts trigger unpleasant feelings, and our bodies pay the price. So, what if we paid attention to these signs and learned from them? We can see emotions as clues about what we are telling ourselves. They tell us when we're beating ourselves up and we need to improve the message. They tell us we're on a dangerous mental track. They'll usually tell us when we're at the wrong party.

Emotions remind us that we're not loving ourselves, and they let us know when we've traveled too far from the truth. The truth may not be something we can put into words, but if we're sober enough to pay attention, we can feel its resonance. We can feel it as love. Take away our words, our preoccupations and obsessive thoughts, and love is all that's left.

What is love? Love is *life*'s energy, creating more *life* all the time and in infinite ways. Most of us were taught to think of love as one kind of emotion—one

among many others. We think that it has a beginning and an end, as emotions usually do. Emotion is
the energy that our bodies create, and love is the sum
of all emotions. Love is energy, and therefore it has
no beginning or end. Energy has no agenda. Neither
does love. It has no limits or conditions. Like all
energy, love can be transformed, but never destroyed.

Unconditional love can seem intimidating at first.
You may want to run from it. You may doubt its
sincerity. You may wonder how it comes so naturally
to children, but not to you. You may want to blame
love for your pain and your self-rejection—but love
is never to blame. What makes things painful and
complicated are the terms and conditions we put on
love. No one wants to hear, "I love you *if* . . ."

"I love you if you can be like me and think like
me." "I love you if you feel my pain." These words
sound funny, but for most people it's the underlying
romantic message. The word *if* denies the truth of
love. "If you loved me, you'd suffer the way I'm suffering," is too often what we mean to say to a loved
one. "If you really cared, you'd make sacrifices for

me," is implied in different ways. "If you truly loved me, you'd prove it, you'd tell your friends, you'd put me first, you'd . . ." Those words may never be spoken, but they tend to hide behind other words. They echo the voice of the main character.

Love doesn't require sacrifice. We are generous in love because we want to be, and we need nothing in return. It's exhilarating to be alive. It's a privilege to feel the power of love. Like *life*, love is its own justification. And, like *life*—like truth—it doesn't need proof in order to exist.

Conditions make love something it isn't, but that's the way we were shown how to love. Conditional love has become part of how we govern ourselves. It forces us to judge people and to demean ourselves. Like any crime, it hurts the body first. It leaves us feeling alone and unwanted, which leads to injuries we're at a loss to fix.

Real love starts with us. It's never too late to rediscover the power of it in ourselves. It's never too late to ask the question, "What is love?" and open all our senses to the answer. Real love has nothing to do with vanity or self-importance. Self-love isn't egotism. The ego is *me*, wanting attention and adulation. Love is the energy that runs through us and all around us. When we share love, we're sharing our *life* force. When we give ourselves love, we're acknowledging what we really are.

When we nurture affection and respect for our human body, the seeds of love begin to grow. We're loving ourselves when we give the body the benefit of every doubt. We're respecting ourselves when we treat the mind like our creation—because it is. If we monitor our thoughts, we can better understand the mind's language. We can become respectful diplomats, softening our words and encouraging the best friend we'll ever have. We can be patient and attentive for the sake of a great love affair.

Your body is the love of your life. The relationship you have with your body affects all relationships. Loving yourself, without conditions, can heal the biggest divisions in your world. It can reconnect you to the force of energy that made your world possible.

15

The Love of Your Life

YOUR PHYSICAL BODY is, and has always been, your true love. There is not, nor will there ever be, a more loyal friend or a more intimate partner. What you think, it will feel. What you command, it will do its best to obey. If you do something to harm your body—including obsessive thinking—it will do everything it can to repair itself. Your body works hard to stay healthy and to make your world easier to tolerate. Out of gratitude for its remarkable generosity, you may want to be generous as well. You can love your body, no matter what. You can put it first in almost every situation. Listening to the needs of your human body may take some practice, but attention is what it needs most.

The mind may want things, but it doesn't need things. Does your body need to feel important? Does it need to gossip? Not at all. The mind is hungry for stories. When we binge on food, we're not making the body happy; we're giving comfort to an agitated mind. The body doesn't need regular sedation, but we routinely try to shut the mind off with alcohol and drugs. We avoid self-reflection by judging others. We deny love, and our bodies suffer.

Loving our bodies unconditionally is natural to us, as we can see from observing small children. Babies and toddlers love without shame or restraint. Over time, children learn to think, to imitate adult behavior, and to put limits on love. They forget to love fearlessly. Most distressingly, they forget to love themselves.

It may be hard to remember, but we all arrived on earth as babies and loved everything about the body we occupied. We loved everything we saw and sensed. As we grew into active children, our bodies took us on a joyride of physical wonders and sensory experiences. We thrived in this paradise—and then, it seems, we were banished from it.

We were told many stories as we grew up, and we believed them all. A few stories suggested there was something sinful, even ugly, about our bodies. Many stories caused us shame. We learned to blame the body for most of life's disappointments. "It's not my fault," the mind learned to say. "I'm only human." But the mind isn't the human body; it's made of virtual stuff. It governs the body in whatever way it's allowed to.

How many of us were taught to love our bodies? Health trends come and go, but listening to your body is a different skill. Where is your attention when you eat, when you exercise, when you're preparing to sleep? Most of the time, it's on past regrets and future worries. You're arguing with people who aren't there. You're anxious about things that aren't happening.

Your physical body, like a child or a lover, needs your attention in order to thrive. It needs a one-on-one conversation now and then. It needs to hear some gratitude for all it does. "I'm so fat!" doesn't provide comfort at all, particularly when the words are spoken with loathing. "I look just like Mom!" sends confusing signals, but eventually your body registers the pain of disappointment. We aren't always thrilled with the way we look, but our bodies aren't at fault.

Our bodies glow when they feel love. They're energized when they feel the truth expressed in action and words. They perform well when we feed them well. They strut when we dress them up. They breathe and bounce when we let them take us for a stroll, a bike ride, or a swim. That's the way we would normally describe a pet—and most of us are far more concerned about the health and happiness of our pets than our own bodies. We're activists when it comes to giving our dogs nutritious food or runs in the doggie park. For some reason, we can't commit to loving our bodies in the same way.

The human body serves us in ways we can't imagine. It compensates for our offenses and keeps on going. It overlooks our crimes. It heals itself—often before we know we're sick. Emotions are important; they maintain the health and metabolism of the body in much the same way that weather patterns balance the planet's metabolism. But the body, doing countless jobs to sustain our health, can be overwhelmed by the drama. It has to support so much indignation, outrage, and fear—and rise to our highest joys. It has to support our convictions and superstitions. And it has to support our absurd theories about love.

Unconditional love *is* love. Everything else is a distortion of love. Love is not one emotion, but the totality of every emotion. It is the force of *life*, and how can we put conditions on that? The body is our home on earth. It gives us all it can give, and we can do the same. Maybe we never learned how to love our physical selves, but it's not too late.

We may adore our cats and goldfish more than we love the human body we inhabit—but, by getting to know that body, we may find ourselves falling in love again.

So it may be time to look at yourself with the eyes of a lover.

16

Lovers and Sweethearts

ROMANTIC LOVE IS considered a different kind
of love. But is it? Your sweetheart's body is your
wonderland, right? True love sees only beauty and
perfection, and a dedicated lover would go to any
length to express that love. If the one you loved
wanted you near, you'd be quick to respond. If you
knew you were missed, you'd call or make the time
to be there physically—or at least you'd give reas-
surances. If your true love was feeling neglected,

you'd offer a hug or plan a date night. You'd apologize for being distracted or for thinking only of yourself.

Well, your body misses you most of the time. It misses the truth. And yes, you're distracted. You're thinking of your reputation and your social status. You're thinking of the last conversation or the next one. You make the minimal effort for your body and often push it beyond its limits. Is exercise a gesture of love or a punishment? What about dieting? If your body isn't feeling your judgment, it's feeling your indifference. Where are the pats and squeezes? Where are the flowers, the love letters?

Self-love is romantic love. When we care deeply for someone, every gesture is an act of love. When we love without condition, there's no impulse to accuse or to resent. Our love doesn't diminish because of judgments made against us. Our love is the very essence of who we are—it is our *life* force. Why would we neglect our bodies, then? Let your body experience all the beauty and wonder around you. When you are embracing *life* fully and appreciating your body for all that it lets you feel, then you are cherishing your closest friend and intimate.

Everyone feels good around people who have genuine love for themselves. It feels heartening, even inspiring, to be in their company. It feels safe. It would be wonderful if people had those same feelings when they're around us. It's not likely to happen if we don't feel comfortable with ourselves.

Once again, we can't give what we don't have. If we have no money to spare, we can't share our wealth. We can't inspire courage if we're always afraid. So it makes sense that loving others is difficult if we don't love ourselves.

Like any love affair, self-love needs nurturing. How do we assure the body that it's loved? We give it the company it needs, of course—not just from other humans but from our story's main character. *Me* needs to get involved in a caring way. *Me* needs to say a kind word now and then. In time, little gestures of appreciation become automatic. In time, we'll wake up every day whispering words of encouragement. We'll see ourselves in a mirror and say something nice. Like any pet or child, the body yearns for tender sounds and intimate assurances. It loves shameless gestures of affection.

There are things you can do for your body, beginning today. You can write love letters to yourself and read them out loud. Devote some time to conversations between the mind and the body. Listen, and reassure. Offer the pat, the squeeze, and the hug now and then. Place a hand on your cheek and wrap the other hand around your shoulder. Hold yourself for a while. Feel better? Of course. Hugs are wonderful, whatever you may have told yourself. This may be the first time since childhood that you acknowledged your body's fundamental need to be touched and appreciated—by you.

Be good company for your body. Take an afternoon nap or have a quiet lunch out alone. Go to the movies together. Commune with *life* by taking a walk in a forest or on a beach. Take a quiet moment to watch the nighttime sky. Give it lots of music! Your mind will appreciate the lyrics, and your body will sway to the beat, the melody, the reverberations of *life*. The body's most important relationship is with *life*, not with your nagging thoughts. Your body is the perfect merging of matter and energy. Your body is the most real thing you know.

You can do better at loving, beginning with the one you literally cannot live without. Say, "I love you," to your body. Say it often, and say it out loud. Say it because it's true. Say it when you start your day. As you settle into bed at night, place your hand on your head and say how much you love your brain and everything connected to the brain. "I love my brain, my ears, my eyes, my nose." Move your hand down to the mouth, the neck, the chest, the shoulders. Name every part of your body as you go, and give thanks to the parts you can't name. Go all the way down to the feet, to the toes. This ritual doesn't take very long, and its effects are powerful.

All of this may feel odd at first, but expressing love is what humans crave. We want to feel it pouring out of us, but we've convinced ourselves that no one wants to receive it. Our bodies definitely do. Everyone's body does, even if their system of government denies it. We love, because love is the energetic force of us. Saying "I love you" brings us back to the truth.

Sex with another human being is also an act of self-love, giving your body what it needs and enjoys. When we make physical love, the voice in our heads goes silent and our stories are forgotten. *Me* is irrelevant—for a time. Loving ourselves causes the same energetic reaction.

Unconditional love for ourselves is the definition of paradise—we began there, remember? The love of your life is not your spouse, your lover, or your child. It's your physical body, your wonderland. Loving your human body makes it possible—even easy—to love all humans the way you were meant to.

Loving requires listening and careful response. Before you go on an angry tirade, consider how it will affect your nervous system. Stop for a moment. Breathe. Step back from the situation and listen to how you're communicating with yourself. Your words are the body's command. Are you making accusations? Are you taking yourself too seriously? If everything is about *me*, then every event will seem personal. Every comment will need a defensive response. Are you willing to do that to your body?

For certain, you can use your energies more productively. You can love without worrying about getting something out of it. Your body will be so grateful. You'll be surprised to find that loving comes naturally. You may discover that you're very generous and that your generosity inspires gratitude in everyone who knows you. Gratitude inspires generosity, which inspires more gratitude. This perfectly describes love in action.

Gratitude and generosity create the ideal relationship between your mind and body. Kindness and affection stimulate your whole system. A little praise brings great emotional reward. Why not let it come from the one telling the story?

Don't let your thoughts hide from you, growing in darkness until they're too strong to control. When you don't have to defend your opinions, you're free to be authentic. You're free to say no, without penalty. You're free to say yes, without regret. You're free to love without limits. You're free to surrender to *life*, to love. It's not the physical body that surrenders; it's the mind giving up its stories. The surrendered mind softens its own laws or throws them out altogether. It allows love to rule, with no interference. In fact, everything changes when the main character respects and reveres the body.

When we love ourselves completely, we return to the place we only knew in infancy. We remember that love has no conditions and needs no justifications. We remember the sensation of paradise and desire only that. Paradise is home, and it's never too late to for us to go back.

17

Love for Humanity

THE WAY BACK to self-love begins when the mind breaks its own spell. Our beliefs act like a fortress, defending us from new insights, but beliefs are made of mist and fog. When there is nothing left to defend, truth is all there is. All the great messengers have recognized this. Their wisdom was evident in their authenticity. Throughout the ages, the most authentic humans have left the brightest legacies.

Wise men and women distinguish themselves by challenging what they know. At some point, they decide to take a deeper look at reality, questioning the world they've created in their minds. They dare to see what is, not what they were taught to see. They refrain from telling old stories and confirming common beliefs. They refuse to let memory dictate reality. They remove the blinders and start a journey toward awareness.

Searching for truth is everyone's birthright and often starts with doubt. "I thought I knew myself, but now I'm not sure. What should I believe? Why should I believe anything?" Doubt begins a process of exploration, as we take another look at the things we were taught to accept as true. "I used to have a theory about life. . . . Was any of it real?"

Doubt can dismantle a belief structure, if we're willing to let it. Why should we do that? Because we want to clear away the nonsense and see the truth. Doubt gives us a chance to look around, observe the crazy party, and decide how we want to play within it. It gives us a chance to revise the main character, whose voice still lingers in our heads—a voice that may not have changed since childhood.

You've grown up. You're not a frightened child anymore. You want to be mature, emotionally and spiritually. You want to be authentic, because acting the part of the main character has made you weary. Doubt reveals your lies. It discredits your stories, until you're ready to cast them aside and put complete faith in the truth of you.

The solution to all conflict is respect. Respect means the end to war, to abuses, and to the kinds of crimes you routinely commit against yourself. Respect brings peace to your world. Self-respect will eventually rewrite the laws that hurt your body. It will transform your congress and your constitution. The old style of leadership will change for the good of your country. There will be no more confused intentions, because words, your best ambassadors, will deliver a clear message. They will offer comfort to your adversaries as well as to your friends.

Respect means you honor the right of every country, or body, to exist—beginning with your own. If other nations can't respect you in turn, they are welcome to find other allies. You won't interfere with their governments, and they needn't interfere with yours.

Respect sounds like a simple solution, but most of us haven't made it a practice. Our defenses are in overdrive. It takes deliberate acts of self-love to overturn our own habits. It takes an internal revolution to rise above our own knowledge.

The earth is the result of billions of years of evolution. The world's governments are the result of thousands of years of evolution. Your little government is barely as old as you are, but your words and actions may well have an influence on future generations.

Consider that when you wonder who you are and how you'd like to affect your world. The president of your little regime can make life a prison or a paradise. Every passing moment gives you a chance to decide on your style of leadership. Whom you vote for—the dictator or the enlightened decision maker—makes all the difference.

Me is never the same, because our impression of reality keeps changing. This means *me* can be as flexible as reality itself. *Me* can be president of an all-inclusive reality, not just the parts that are comfortable and familiar. The main character can rescue the body or rule it recklessly. It can be taught to doubt automatic assumptions and resist the temptation to repeat them. With practice, self-importance begins to seem unnatural. Self-pity loses its appeal, and we stop taking things so personally.

Right now you're reading or hearing these words read aloud. This means you're converting spoken symbols into mental imagery. The words have no life of their own until you read or hear them. They're dead things until imagination brings them to life.

Once you imagine something, it's alive in a virtual landscape. You read, listen, and create a world to exist in. Now these words and their meanings can be applied to your actions. If you choose, you can make ideas come to life in the world of people and places. This is how you built your personal reality in the first place—you watched, learned, and let desire drive you. You built real things out of ideas. You used the powers of attention, memory, and imagination to become a unique human in the human dream.

Like setting up an avatar in a video game, we choose the character we want to be. We dress it up and arm it with weapons or strategies for survival. Through the centuries we've used books, plays, and movies to enjoy realities that we're not able to play out in our own lives. Today's video technology makes it possible to interact with characters we create—as well as those created by people we may never meet. What we may not realize is that we've been doing this for ourselves all along—without books, without technology.

In life, it takes years to build the character you know as *me*. No one is born with an intellectual sense of self. As babies, we just are. We see, we sense, and we respond in whatever ways we can. As we learn to use words and give them meaning, we begin to describe ourselves. Of course, we get a lot of assistance—the people around us, already adept at explaining things, are eager to tell us who we are. They describe us according to their judgments, their hopes, and how they see themselves in us.

So, little by little, we begin to imagine *me*. We all know how kids like to play with ideas of themselves. A small child can spend an entire day as a dog, barking and begging for treats. Children become knights and princesses in their imaginations, creating environments to go along with those roles. They build fortresses and treetop castles. They imagine entire kingdoms and rule them confidently. We all remember playing with imaginary friends, but the imaginary friend who follows us everywhere, and always, is *me*.

As a community, humanity tells classic stories of heroes and gods. In the story we tell about ourselves, each of us is the hero—the fallen hero or the savior. We are victors or persecuted victims, according to our stories. We seem self-reliant or helpless, depending on how much attention we crave. Our hairstyles and outfits change with the times, but beliefs and behaviors eventually settle in to stay—until we choose to wake up, to truly look at ourselves, and to change what doesn't work.

Our habitual behavior "doesn't work" when it pushes away the people we love. A belief doesn't work if it makes us feel bad. An ideology doesn't work if it leads to obsession, fear, or cynicism.

We've been using the power of imagination to define ourselves throughout our lives. We can use that power again in order to be the best possible person within the context of any dream. It's important to see where we are now and how we got here. Think about the transformative events of your life. They may not be the ones that family photos have documented. They might have happened when you were alone; they might have happened without your notice. You had a thought, you imagined the world differently for a second, and everything changed.

Change is frequently the result of subtle realizations. You read a book or you see a movie. Something changes your viewpoint or awakens your curiosity. You listen in on another conversation, and it causes you to reflect on your life. You hear a song whose lyrics go straight to your heart, and nothing is the same afterward.

Incidents like these might have changed the course of your life. They might have nudged you in a new direction or given you direction when you had none. Maybe you followed expectations or walked a path that was already laid out for you. However events unfolded, they brought you to this point, this moment.

Life is teaching us all the time. We are all apprentices in that sense, and we can create any kind of discipline for ourselves. We can set aside a few minutes every day to remind ourselves of the truth—to breathe calmly, listen to our internal voices, and dismiss them. Our thoughts document this day's events, yesterday's events, and idly speculate about future events. They're not telling us anything new or anything that's true.

The stories that we tell about this life are fiction. *Me* is the protagonist in this work of fiction. When *me* believes its worst stories, fear and paranoia rule the human body. Then it seems that a demon has been unleashed. All stories about spiritual warriors have tried to illustrate this. The final confrontation with *me* is the key element in sacred stories. The story of the Buddha illustrates this beautifully. Denouncing *me* as an illusion is the act of a spiritual master. The story of Jesus meeting *me* in the desert is a classic lesson in awareness. Your creation may be not seem like a devil or a saint, but to make it aware of itself takes conscious effort. All traditions tell the same story, each with its own symbols and characters.

The mind's world is built upon a bedrock of symbols, and it's important to distinguish the ways every symbol explains what is real. It's important to see how every human mind uses imagination to create its own version of reality. Actually, every mind creates a version of *unreality*. Every mind creates its own virtual world. It can also re-create it. It can scan its own database of stories, looking for malicious information, and self-correct. It can end the strategy of isolating the human body, alienating it, and then controlling it however it wishes. Judgments and criticisms can go. Gossip and speculation can go. Suspicions and prejudices—all of our excuses to hate—can go.

Representative governments need a system of checks and balances. Our personal knowledge, for all it inspires, should be challenged. Our irrational fears should be faced and resolved. No belief should be allowed to induce shame. In spite of the laws we instituted, we need to be free to love without condition.

18

Fear and Knowledge

ONE OF THE biggest barriers to love is fear. Of course, fear is natural to every organism; it's meant to alert us to danger and preserve our physical lives. Irrational fear, on the other hand, is different. It's the fear of something that doesn't exist. Children can't tell the difference between real and irrational fear, and it's fair to say the rest of us can't either. We have a scary thought and the body reacts, sensing real danger. We detect fear in other people and catch the virus. We observe their reactions and mimic their hysteria. We panic. *What we know* clearly has the power to do us harm.

As children, we didn't question what we knew. We could name the things that scared us—thunder, darkness, hairy spiders. We "knew" there were creatures in the basement without names. We knew those creatures were real, because we were terrified of them; and we knew we were terrified, because those creatures were real.

Even now, we know when we are afraid, and we know why. Knowing encourages more fear, and fear confirms what we know. This sounds a like an endless cycle, doesn't it? So we must challenge our knowledge. And we have to face fear sooner or later. The longer we wait, the bigger the fears get.

Facing fear brings clarity. Clarity, in turn, reduces fear—allowing us to turn off our bedroom light without worrying about demons in the shadows or ogres under the bed. What is real? Not our irrational fears, and not the stories we have so long believed about ourselves and our relationship with *life*.

Admitting what is *not real* takes us a long way toward personal awareness.

We know that beliefs adapt to new circumstances; they change and fade away. The more we accept a belief as a choice, the less power our fears have over us. With less fear, our confidence strengthens; and with more confidence, the better we get at challenging our beliefs. We see what they are, and we know instinctively they're not real. We can discard them if we want. We also know when we've stopped being afraid. We know when we're happy, and when we feel safe. So *what we know,* in that sense, can also save us.

First, we need to accept that we're afraid. Fear often runs under the radar, and only our actions give us a clue. Challenging fear means finding its source and then looking deeper. This means excuses aren't acceptable. "Well, my mom used to say . . ." doesn't justify the beliefs that follow us into adulthood. "I've been like this ever since my accident . . ." doesn't explain why we're still afraid and unhappy. "I've been told I'm high-strung," usually means we've made peace with our anxieties.

We hold on to fear for many reasons. We hold on to old beliefs because they've become comfortable. Change is inconvenient and brings too many surprises. We want things to stay the same. We want our phobias to define us. In many cases, we don't know who we'd be without our fears. It could also be that we just never got around to telling them good-bye.

If we're ready to change, there are things we can do. We can be a lot more honest with ourselves, for one. We can confess our attachment to fear or to the beliefs that cause us fear. It often helps to listen to other people talk through their fears. Offering someone else comfort is helpful too. We used to do this intuitively as children—taking a friend's hand on a dark road or comforting a puppy through a thunderstorm.

We can still help a child check for goblins under the bed. We can look under our own "bed." We may have been imagining the worst, only to discover that the worst isn't so bad. We can face our own fear for the sake of a friend. Friends can face goblins together. They can grow and become stronger by giving each other confidence.

Fear, left unchallenged, controls our lives and leads our actions. We often say we're afraid of other people—a partner, a boss, a stranger. In most cases, we're afraid our own reactions. We're afraid of how *me* might react to any given situation. We're afraid of what we'll do next to disappoint, confuse, or betray ourselves. Whatever the reason, we're afraid—and it must be somebody's fault.

When we blame events, people, or God for our problems, we're playing the role of a victim. Like those primitive hunters on a moonless night, we're helpless to save ourselves. Anger doesn't make us more capable. Self-pity wins us no admiration. When we separate ourselves from the problem, we get farther away from a solution. The fact is, we are the problem. We are the confusion, through no fault of our own. And we are also the only solution.

To wake up and see is the gift we give ourselves. To do something about what we see is our salvation. Awareness is *life*'s gift to mortals. Hercules might have prayed to Zeus for gifts of power, but only he, Hercules, could decide how to use power wisely.

No matter what we do in life, we are all explorers seeking truth. We listen for truth in classic stories and common conversations. We evolve as individuals when we challenge ourselves to see. Humanity evolves when we challenge what we know. People once believed the sun revolved around this planet. We were certain that if we traveled far enough, we'd drop off the earth. We knew what we feared. We feared what we knew.

The mind builds its own house out of illusions— bright ones and dreary ones—from the time we start to talk and think. Everything goes along smoothly until expectations are crushed. Everything seems great until our desires conflict with other people's desires. Everything is fine until our unshakable reality is shaken, and then panic sets in. Rigid beliefs will break soon enough.

When a virtual earthquake happens, the body trembles and emotions burst to the surface. We all know this, because we've lived through it many times. We say we've been disappointed in love or betrayed by a friend, and we've reacted. We've acted out.

Thinking they're helping, loved ones support our worst stories. They confirm our worst fears. They too become outraged and suggest we seek some kind of revenge—and we listen to them.

The more we commit to the story, the harder it is to see clearly. The less we see, the more afraid we are. The more afraid we are, the more we cling to our stories. Knowledge and fear work hand in hand. As we become more irrational, the body suffers even more.

Old ideas and bad habits will continue to hurt us if we're unable to give ourselves some grace. A heartbreak can last a lifetime if we don't recognize the gift it brings. If a lover disappoints or rejects us, we feel heartbroken. If we have to leave a beloved school, we're heartbroken. If a belief is disproved or our image of someone destroyed, we're heartbroken—but it's not the heart that breaks. What breaks is the mind's absolute certainty. What gets threatened is the main character, so sure of *me*. When the virtual reality receives a blow, the body responds in shock.

The thing people call heartbreak is the result of a head-on collision with truth. This is a perfect opportunity for real awareness. "It didn't turn out the way I'd imagined," we might say to ourselves. "She's not the person I thought she was." "He's not the man I married." These are often said with sadness and grief, but they are important revelations. In them, we hear the doubt in *me*. Its reality has been challenged. This is when the mind has a chance to face itself and see its own illusions. Love doesn't hurt us. Love isn't to blame for our pain, and love is never an excuse to suffer.

Nobody is to blame, whatever the drama. We're being given a chance to see what actually is rather than what we wanted to imagine. This is a good thing, but the typical response to disappointment is to become spiteful. We pity ourselves and want everyone else to pity us. This hurts the body and puts more distance between what is real and what we imagine to be real. In other words, we're lying to ourselves again.

We get disappointed when others can't live up to

our fantasies of them. Friends fail to meet our expectations, and we feel cheated. Lovers can't measure up to our standards, and we feel rejected. People aren't what we think they are, but is it ever their fault? We wanted to imagine them our way, no matter what the evidence said to the contrary. Instead of feeling self-pity, we can feel gratitude for the chance to awaken. Instead of focusing on what wasn't there, we can begin to focus on what is.

We all learned to get attention by telling a good story. Attention is what we all enjoy, and telling a dramatic story is a great way to get it. We've learned just what parts to tell a particular audience. We've made them laugh. We've made them cry. We're accomplished at drawing other people into our life's drama, because we believe it.

We identify ourselves through our stories, and when a story is challenged, we feel threatened. "If this isn't true, what else about me isn't true?" we wonder. "If I'm not me, then who am I?" If one thing is false, then nothing can be true. The body hears those messages and feels anxious. "Who's driving this machine?" it could justifiably wonder. "And where are we going?"

People come from different cultures, but we all have one thing in common. We direct precious energy into being who we say we are. We get distracted and wander from the truth. We let fear control us. We dodge questions and give alibis. That isn't spiritual maturity, or maturity of any kind. But, like the children we once were, we can face our fear. We can walk through existence in a way we never thought we could. We can grow up.

We can change the rules we live by, because we created those rules. We can see *life* in its totality, not through the "eyes" of one predictable character. Anyone can learn to see, explore, and discover what's real. Like hungry tourists in a foreign country, any of us can acquire a taste for exotic things. In other words, the mind can develop a taste for truth.

Does it want to? As long as we believe we're accurately representing the truth, why should we crave a different taste? Why can't we just be drunk and stay that way? Well, think about that for a second.

Drunks of any kind don't really like themselves, and they don't see much to like about life. They lie to the people close to them, and they deceive themselves. Drunks are what we've been, and now we want something else.

Most drunks would probably rather be sober. They'd rather see clearly, breathe fresh air, and feel the sun on their faces. They'd rather feel the touch of truth and not just speculate about it.

They want to be the best humans they can be, but how can they do that?

19

Peace in Our Time

THERE'S A REASON these pearls of wisdom follow important questions. Questions are invitations. They are preludes to action. They offer a chance to break through fears and barriers of accepted knowledge.

Sometimes we hear an idea that's strange to our ears, but it still resonates as truth. We get excited, and we want more. We listen closer or read further. We rearrange our thinking to include that perspective. A new theory sets us on a philosophical adventure, and, like any adventure, it has its scary elements. If we take this ride, we'll almost certainly end up in a different place. Our view of the world will be transformed, and we'll learn things about ourselves we didn't know before. Yes, it sounds scary, but also exhilarating.

Most of us love to explore new worlds. We love it, until we feel we're losing *me*. Some of us reach a point in our spiritual excursions when we don't recognize ourselves anymore. That's usually when we get scared and end the whole adventure. We give up. We get a little tipsy and return to the party.

If we're willing to keep going, that's when the real adventure begins. That's when *life* starts to play with us—talking to us and calling to us in our dreams. New information starts coming from everywhere. We read things, hear things, and respond to things differently. We look at everything with fresh eyes. The words on that billboard we pass every day start to sound wise. Mindless television commercials reveal secret knowledge. Conversations overheard at restaurants seem to deliver profound messages. Suddenly, we're decoding *life*'s riddles, one at a time.

As any scientist will testify, searching for answers brings unexpected revelations. Curiosity opens unseen doors and offers surprising points of view. We go to sleep with a question and wake up with a new point of view. It's not that the information we get is really new, only that we're suddenly allowing ourselves to receive it.

Life is the bearer of information—by way of words, images, or a hit song on the radio. It speaks the truth to us continuously, tirelessly, mostly without words. Unwilling to master our own attention, we miss a lot. When we're fixated on one thing, we're blind to everything else. When we welcome a different idea, however reluctantly, reality begins to shift. Our imaginations ignite, and we get a glimpse of the truth.

We can imagine eternity, infinity, and immortality. We can sense the magnitude of love's force. We're often transported when imagining God. But if we open our eyes, we see God here in front of us: we see *life* radiating from everything. We witness love in action—everywhere. We feel energy. We sense the eternal and infinite power of us moving through all matter.

Humanity's greatest art is to dream consciously—using language the way a master artist uses brushes and paints. We are the artist of our dream, and we are the central point of focus in whatever landscape we choose to imagine.

We were meant to wake up and see what's all around us. We were designed to change and to evolve. Our physical bodies never stop changing. Energy never stays the same. Still, we attempt to define ourselves the same way through the years of our lives. Would we really rather not wake up?

We all know what it feels like to wake up, since we do it every morning. Eyes still closed, we hear sounds and decipher their meaning. We listen and feel our bodies stir. We sense energy, in and around us, in so many different ways. Taking a conscious breath, we move, stretch, and feel the wonder of being human. Then we open our eyes.

Remember the first time? It's easy to imagine opening our eyes for the first time. We did this as newborns, and we've done it over and over again throughout our lives. Every time we wake from a night's sleep, from a nap—every time we jolt ourselves back from a daydream—we have a chance to see for the first time.

Close your eyes, and the world disappears. Open them again, and everything you see is a miracle. Everything you hear is an intimate vibration of energy, a greeting from *life*. Awake and aware, we can see the world as it is and respond to it authentically. Isn't that easier than having to recall the role you're playing every minute of every day?

When our eyes open, the brain starts to register images, and the mind comes to rapid conclusions—it begins to tell a story. All this happens because light has entered our eyes. All we ever really see is light, in fact. All anyone ever sees is light, touching objects and bouncing off objects. The rest is a story. The rest is a spell cast by a gifted magician. It takes a dedicated sorcerer to break that self-made spell.

It takes someone willing to wake up, to open the senses, and to see.

Everyone is driven by an ongoing dream, and everyone has the power to steer that dream in a new direction. Everyone has a chance to alter the message. *Angel* is another word for messenger. The way we react to people and occurrences makes us the angels we are. We may feel like reluctant angels, disgraced angels, or recovering angels, but we're learning to deliver the message of *life* through our words and our actions. With each revelation, we're becoming more aware of *life*'s message. We're learning to see a broader picture of the world. We're enriching our relationship with all things.

Peace means freedom from disturbance. On a global scale, it means there is no war between nations. It means different cultures get along; their traditions are respected and their beliefs tolerated. Peace means that one government doesn't seek to overthrow or impose its principles on another.

Peace means the same thing to you, to me, and to everyone. It means an end to the chaos in our minds. It means we've ended our war over ideas, a war that causes us confusion and unrest. We don't want to impose our principles on anyone else or to disrespect other people's beliefs and traditions. The peace we create in our time, in our universe, has a lasting influence. It ensures our own sense of well-being, and it affects the safety and well-being of the world around us.

You may be dissatisfied with your life or frustrated with the way things are going right now. You may feel as though you have no control over anything—not your friends, your children, or your reality. Maybe you wonder what makes other people do what they do. Maybe you've realized that you don't know everything, and you can't know everything.

"I don't know" is a game changer. When you give up having to know or needing to be right, you feel lighter right away. Surrender your stories. The mind is not the boss of anything, and it doesn't want to be. Let *life* take over from here.

Life is energy, truth, intent. No image you have of yourself can match the real energy and power of you. Words, no matter how sincerely spoken, can't express the truth. You are energy living inside a human being. You are truth, wrapped up in a fanciful story.

At its core, this is the story of an awakening mind. Like most of us, you can only see yourself one way until you use the power of attention to see much more. You believe one reflection until you learn to see yourself in everything. Trust completely in the truth, and you will feel all your lies fade away.

Most of us trust nature. We feel comfortable in nature, even in a city park. We enjoy the uninhibited company of animals and the serenity of trees. This might seem strange, considering that nature can harm us. Nature can turn violent. It can ravage a forest or bring down a mountain. Animals soil our carpets and bite our relatives. They are both unpredictable and in many ways unreliable. What's so comforting about that? What is there to trust?

What we trust is authenticity. Animals and trees don't hide behind a story. *Life* rules the oceans and mountain ranges; our thoughts don't. We're reluctant to see ourselves as part of nature. Instead, we see ourselves as nature's rivals. We see ourselves as tourists within a natural landscape. As tourists, we wonder and we marvel. We admire the intelligence of trees and the sensitivity of raindrops. We feel that the sea and the sky know something we don't and that nature has a secret power we lack.

There is only *life*, and its countless points of view. It's a disservice to *life*, to truth, to think we are separate from it. It's self-defeating to deny *life*'s power and magic in ourselves.

Whether we're listening to it or not, our internal chatter adds to the stress our bodies are feeling. It affects our moods. It alters the way we deal with other people, and it makes us struggle just to get through the day. So much is going on in our minds that we can hardly make decisions or have clear conversations.

Unable to contain the inner story, we talk about our problems, needs, and frustrations. We voice our opinions too loudly. We pull everyone's attention toward *me*. What we think we know consumes us. What other people know infects us. Our focus is on the news, on speculations, but not the truth. Our bodies get hooked on drama, which only makes us hungrier for more drama, more gossip and conspiracies.

Inwardly, we're punishing ourselves for our misdeeds and blaming ourselves for our misfortunes. We carry memories everywhere we go, even if their weight is unbearable. Our eyes are on the past, and our imaginations fly to the future. This makes us impervious to the present moment. So we forget to be kind. We forget to say hello to a stranger or listen to a friend. We forget to be good to ourselves.

All this can be turned around. We can afford to give love generously—because love is the truth of us. It has no limits. Love is the energy of us. It costs us nothing to respect ourselves without looking for justifications. It costs us nothing to respect everyone we meet, because all matter was created from the same mystery. All humans were born innocent of crimes. All of us survived to this point, bending to unspoken laws and withstanding the noise of our own thoughts.

Out of pure potential we were conceived and created. We survived all the ordeals of childhood and
the pressures of the human dream. And we're here
now, wondering and wanting, because we know there
are things we can still learn. We sense there's a better
way to be human.

We were blessed with a brain and a nervous system that allow us to receive information directly
from *life*. We are able to create a virtual world, instant
by instant. It's not fixed; it's fluid. Our reality can
be reshaped; the human body will respond to new
agreements. Our emotions don't have to respond to
clumsy leadership. Our thoughts can be tempered.
Every one of us is able to reflect the truth through
our words and actions. And that—let's face it—is
an amazing superpower.

20

Afterword

FOR ALL HIS work, the boy in our story went home without coins in his pocket—but that's not why he made such a heroic effort to help an old man with his wagon. He did it for love; he did it because love was the truth of who he was. His every word was a messenger of love from his own little country to an unfamiliar one. He would return home all the better for having built a bridge between two human beings.

As his life unfolded, he would face challenges. He might learn to wage unnecessary wars in his head. He might be expected to join the party of drunks and impose his beliefs on other minds. He might never face his fears or question his own knowledge. His true nature might become corrupted, causing him to fall out of love with himself.

He might also wake up. He might, if he remembered the words of an old man, find his way back to paradise. He might remember to love unconditionally, as one who truly loves himself. He might learn to shape reality like a master artist.

Things are the way they are in the world not because they are right or wrong. Naturally, there are things we can all do better for the sake of our personal happiness. We can free ourselves of our own tyrannies and give ourselves the sense of safety we've been longing for. Because we are free doesn't mean other "countries" will be free. It doesn't mean that other leaders will be aware or responsible. The choice for transformation belongs to every individual. We can guide ourselves toward personal independence, but should not coerce anyone else to follow us. Our journey back to authenticity is ours alone and mustn't be used as an excuse to pressure family members or dear friends.

At any time, we can wake up and see the totality of what we are. We can see *life* as it is and accept everything we see. We can show how truth walks and talks in the world without attempting to govern others. We can offer our presence—not our rules—to demonstrate the best of what a human can be.

We don't have to imagine ourselves more aggressive or more helpless than we are. In fact, we'll be happier if we don't. We'll be more able to meet daily surprises and upheavals without our old illusions. We can be grateful, whatever the disturbance. No matter the circumstances, we can live permanently in paradise. Having already recognized what we are not, we can live each moment as truth, as energy. We can perceive as *life* perceives, enjoying all points of view.

It's up to each of us to appreciate the main character of our story as a work of fiction. It's up to each of us to create a masterpiece by being aware of what is. The voice in our heads is meant to evolve. Through the transformation of the main character, we can have a loving influence on the lives of those around us. We can make words impeccable again. Through *me*, we can transform our personal reality.

So, please, help *me* to change your world.